BUTTERFLIES
of NORTH AMERICA

BUTTERFLIES
of NORTH AMERICA

Jeffrey Glassberg

STERLING

New York / London
www.sterlingpublishing.com

STERLING and the distinctive Sterling logo are registered trademarks
of Sterling Publishing Co., Inc.

2 4 6 8 10 9 7 5 3 1

Published by Sterling Publishing Co., Inc.
387 Park Avenue South, New York, NY 10016

© 2011 by Sterling Publishing Co., Inc.

Distributed in Canada by Sterling Publishing
c/o Canadian Manda Group, 165 Dufferin Street
Toronto, Ontario, Canada M6K 3H6

Distributed in the United Kingdom by GMC Distribution Services
Castle Place, 166 High Street, Lewes, East Sussex, England BN7 1XU

Distributed in Australia by Capricorn Link (Australia) Pty. Ltd.
P.O. Box 704, Windsor, NSW 2756, Australia

Printed in China
All rights reserved

Sterling ISBN 978-1-4027-8620-4

For information about custom editions, special sales, premium and
corporate purchases, please contact Sterling Special Sales
Department at 800-805-5489 or specialsales@sterlingpublishing.com.

Half-title page: A Swamp Metalmark perches on a black-eyed susan.

Title page: A Clodius Parnassian nectars at bindweed.

Contents

Above: Julia Heliconian. **Opposite:** Greenish Blue.

The World of Butterflies

$\mathcal{W}$elcome to the wonderful world of butterflies. It's bursting with color, filled with flowers, and packed with non-stop action. Associated with freedom, spiritual growth, and the human soul, your involvement with butterflies can improve your physical, mental, and spiritual condition. Your growing attraction to butterflies will bring you to some of the most beautiful places on Earth and richly reward you with a lifetime of exhilarating experiences. By focusing on butterflies — small but lavishly beautiful — you will also begin to see other small but splendid parts of nature, like opulent flowers and astounding beetles.

The purpose of this book is to show you how to find and recognize many of the butterflies that you will see in your own neighborhood and throughout the United States, and to provide information about these butterflies.

Because many of the six hundred species found in the Lower 48 states of the United States are very similar to one another, the approach I have taken in this book, with many of these groups, is to allow you to identify an unknown butterfly to group, rather than to species. For example, both greater fritillaries and duskywings are groups of butterflies that perplex experts who try to identify them to species. They sometimes do so incorrectly. So, if you see a butterfly that closely resembles the illustration of a Great Spangled Fritillary (p. 127) or another that resembles a Wild Indigo Duskywing (p. 187), you shouldn't assume that your butterfly is either of these species. Rather, you should conclude that you are viewing a fritillary or a duskywing, respectively. Your answer will be less precise than if you had said "It's a Wild Indigo Duskywing," but it may well be more accurate. If, after experience, you decide that you would like to identify butterflies to specific species, even in difficult groups, then you can use my *Butterflies through Binoculars* series to do so.

The Birth of Butterflying

Early stage naturalists begin the study of a group of organisms by "cataloging" the species that are present. John James Audubon, one of America's most famous naturalists, began bird study in this country by shooting birds and bringing the dead specimens

Everyone gets excited about a rare Pepper and Salt Skipper, even though (or perhaps because) it's only one-half inch long and inconspicuous. Watching butterflies with other people is part of the fun of butterflying, as is the chance to capture the butterfly's image on film.

back to his studio for study. Likewise, in the 1800s, early butterfly enthusiasts, most notably William Edwards in West Virginia and Samuel Scudder in Boston, collected butterflies with nets and pored over the dead specimens to determine the different types of butterflies that inhabited the country.

Moving into the 20th century, in the 1920s members of the Bronx Bird Club realized that affordable binoculars, developed during World War I, could be used to identify birds, eliminating the need to shoot them. An associate of the group, Roger Tory Peterson, based his first bird guide, published in 1934, upon this approach — identifying birds in the field using "field marks" rather than in a lab or museum, using a technical manual.

When Peterson expanded the field guide series, he approached fellow Connecticut resident Alexander B. Klots to write a butterfly guide. In a conversation I had with him at his house in Old Lyme, I asked Peterson why he didn't have Klots write a real field guide rather than a manual intended to help identify dead butterflies. Peterson replied that Klots told him that such an approach was not feasible for butterflies and, given the lack of appropriate binoculars and the somewhat limited state of our knowledge of butterflies at that time (1950), Klots was probably right. The few butterfly books that were published subsequent to Klots' work continued to approach butterfly identi-fication as the identification of dead butterflies. Although, in the 1970s Robert Michael Pyle worked to increase public involvement with butterflies, into the 1980s butterflies remained the province of a small group of collectors.

In 1984, a group of butterfly enthusiasts in New York City, led by Guy Tudor, formed the New York City Butterfly Club. Modern butterflying began soon afterward, in 1985, when club member Steve Walter discovered Minolta pocket binoculars, to my knowledge the first close-focusing binoculars. Members of the club had already realized that most butterflies could be identified in the field, without nets, and the availability of close-focusing binoculars now freed these first butterfliers from the need for nets.

By the late 1980s, the lack of an acceptable guidebook that actually allowed one to identify butterflies in the field had become intolerable. Since none was in the offing, I set about to create one myself. The result was *Butterflies through Binoculars: A Field Guide to Butterflies in the Boston-New York-Washington Region*, published in 1993.

Also in 1993, the North American Butterfly Association (NABA) was founded to promote public enjoyment and conservation of butterflies. (See the appendix for more information about NABA.) More recently, *Butterflies through Binoculars: East* and *Butterflies through Binoculars: West* were published and these now allow, for the first time, almost any butterfly found in the United States to be identified in the field.

Binoculars

The majority of butterflies are actually quite small. Using one's eyes alone one can see a tiny flash of orange that is an American Copper, but not much more. Although one can certainly enjoy butterflies using only the naked eye, binoculars greatly increase one's ability to see all of the colors, sheens, and intricate patterns that make butterflies so sensational. Binoculars enhance one's enjoyment by enlarging the image of the butterfly: depending upon the type used, the image will appear to be seven to ten times closer than it is.

However, most binoculars do not work well for butterflying. That is because when one is standing, for example, five feet away from a butterfly, this is too close for most binoculars to focus properly, resulting in an unviewably blurry image. For butterflying, one wants close-focusing binoculars, that is, binoculars that will allow one to see a sharp image even when the butterfly one is viewing is closer than six feet away. Some close-focusing binoculars allow one to approach to almost three feet and still see a sharp image.

When purchasing binoculars there are many factors to consider. Probably the two most important are the already mentioned close-focusing feature (just how close can

A group of butterfliers keep their binoculars within easy reach as they take part in a NABA 4th of July Butterfly Count in Westchester County, New York.

With spectacular scenery as a backdrop, Glacier National Park, Montana, has special butterflies not found elsewhere in the United States. Here, butterfliers use binoculars to scan the fields for likely butterfly locations.

you get) and the power of the binoculars (how much bigger will the image be). The power of the binoculars is given as the first of two numbers that traditionally describe binoculars, for example, a pair of binoculars described as 8 x 42 will be 8 power, or 8x, binoculars. In general, more power is good. But there are also downsides to power. All other things being equal, the more powerful the binoculars are, the more difficult it is to aim them and to hold them steady. In addition, more powerful binoculars will often weigh more. If you are not experienced with binoculars, my recommendation would be to use 7x binoculars.

Other factors include field of view (the wider the field of view, the easier it is to find the butterfly in the binoculars), weight (you're going to be carrying these around a lot), and light-gathering ability. The latter is affected by the diameter of the objective lens (larger is brighter), which is the second of the two given numbers, for example, 42 in the 8 x 42, and by the quality and coating of the lenses. And of course, for most people, price is another important factor.

For the latest information about binoculars, visit the NABA website where binocular reviews are posted. After reviewing all the information, if possible, test suggested binoculars yourself; many factors (such as handling) are subjective, and deciding which binoculars are "best" is a matter of personal preference.

Finding Butterflies

WHERE TO FIND BUTTERFLIES

Although butterflies seem very fragile, they are sturdy enough to be found almost everywhere on our planet. The greatest variety is found in the steaming rain forests of the Amazon basin, but butterflies also live in the deserts, on the tops of our tallest mountains, in the vast and treeless expanses of the arctic tundra, and, of course, in your backyard.

So, your own backyard isn't a bad place to start looking. Turn to the butterfly gardening section for advice on how to increase the number of butterflies near your home. At some point, you'll probably want to explore regions a little farther afield. One of the great joys of butterflying is learning the locations of all the little nooks and crannies in your neighborhood that serve as interesting natural habitats.

As you search for butterflies, it is helpful to keep in mind what butterflies like. Most like flowers. Learn the important wild nectar sources in your region (see the table on page 42 for a beginning list). Then, when you see a stand of these plants, you will know to check them for nectaring butterflies.

Most butterflies like sunshine. When you are butterflying, you should be drenched with sunshine. Look for open areas with natural vegetation. Wet meadows, dry meadows, prairie, oak savannas, brushland. These are all productive butterfly habitats.

Butterflying can take you from coast to coast, and everywhere in between. **Above:** The author sits astride a horse at an altitude of more than 12,000 feet in the Wind River Mountains of Wyoming, searching for Mountain Fritillaries. **Inset:** Butterfliers stop along a road in the Lower Rio Grande Valley of Texas, and find many unusual species at a flowering shrub.

Rhododendron forest in the fog belt along the northern California coast; the area is home to Great Arctics and Mardon Skippers.

Rhododendron forest in western North Carolina; the area is home to Tawny Crescents.

Most like complexity. Fields filled with only a very few types of plants will not have many different species of butterflies. Look for areas with a great diversity of plants. Even better, look for areas where different habitats come together. A wet meadow adjacent to a dry meadow is more productive than either one alone. An area where a wet meadow meets a dry meadow at the edge of an oak woodland is a butterflier's paradise.

One strategy for locating suitable areas is simply to travel along the roads near where you live, stopping whenever you see a likely spot. Another approach is to find powerline right-of-ways or unused railroad beds, and follow these as they slice through suitable habitat. A bonus to this method is that the powerline cuts and railroad beds themselves are often excellent habitats for butterflies.

Look on a map of your region and locate state, county, and local parks. These areas, if they are not too manicured, may well provide good butterfly habitats. Contact the state or local office of the Nature Conservancy and find out where their preserves are located. These important natural areas are often home to a variety of butterflies. Or, locate issues of *American Butterflies*. Most issues have descriptions of top butterflying locations.

BUTTERFLY CONCENTRATORS

Now that you've found some likely looking habitats for butterflies, it's time to look for the butterflies themselves. Sometimes, butterflies are everywhere, by the thousands. But many times, the numbers of butterflies are much smaller. When this is the case, one wants to find features of the environment that concentrate the butterflies. Here are a few suggestions.

Finding flowers is usually your best bet for finding butterflies. **Above left:** An orange milkweed is thronged by Pearl Crescents and one Acadian Hairstreak. **Above right:** Orange Sulphurs find a common milkweed to their taste. **Below:** Large groups of mudpuddling butterflies can be thrilling. Here, at least seven species — Tailed Orange, Sleepy Orange, Mimosa Yellow, Mexican Yellow, Southern Dogface, Large Orange Sulphur, and Lyside Sulphur — cluster at damp sand.

Flowers: Of course, I've already mentioned flowers. But their importance in finding and observing butterflies cannot be overemphasized. As an aid to finding butterflies, learning the most important wild nectar sources for butterflies is invaluable.

Hilltops: See the behavior section for an explanation of hilltopping. Locating accessible hilltops is useful almost everywhere and especially important throughout the west.

Mudpuddles: Damp sand or gravel attracts many butterflies. Look for places where dirt roads cross streams, or along a stream where there is wet sand.

A good place to find butterflies such as White Peacocks and Ruddy Daggerwings is a patch of Spanish needles, where they like to nectar, such as those lining part of the boardwalk at Royal Palm Hammock, Everglades National Park, Florida. If you're really lucky, a big Palatka Skipper will show up.

Trails: Not only are butterflies easier to see along a trail, the trail itself serves to concentrate some of them. Believe it or not, many butterflies, such as buckeyes, prefer trails to untrammeled vegetation.

WHEN TO FIND BUTTERFLIES

Most butterflies like it warm and sunny. Thus for successful butterflying you generally want a sunny day with a temperature of greater than about 60°F. The hotter the day, the less critical sunshine becomes. Although there are certainly exceptions, most butterflies don't really fly until after 9 A.M. In many locations and at many times of the year, there is little activity before 10 A.M. Relax and have a leisurely breakfast.

Activity wanes late in the afternoon. But some species habitually come down from the treetops to nectar at low flowers at this time of day, so this is a good time to search for them.

Identifying Butterflies

WHY IDENTIFY BUTTERFLIES?

For many people, a legitimate question might be "Why should I bother to identify butterflies at all? I don't need to know their names to enjoy them." And, of course, there is much truth to this. Knowing how to identify all 600 or so species of United States butterflies doesn't necessarily mean that you enjoy the actual butterflies any more than someone who loves watching the tiger swallowtails in their garden but can't identify them by name. In fact, some people who keep long lists of the different kinds of butterflies they see probably enjoy the listing process more than the butterflies themselves. But learning to recognize the many different species of butterflies along with their names can enhance your enjoyment of the butterflies themselves. How? Well, think of people.

You can enjoy people whom you don't know, but because each individual is different, when you know someone's name it's easier to attach details to that individual. One person you recognize likes spinach strudel while another refuses to eat broccoli. Each group of butterfly species also has its own characteristics. So while on one level you can enjoy two white butterflies interacting in your garden, perhaps it adds something to know that one is a Cabbage White, a widespread, introduced species that flies throughout warm weather and eats a large variety of plants (including broccoli), while the other is an orangetip, a native species that flies only in the early spring and eats only rock cresses and related plants (no broccoli for these guys). When you notice that the flight of one is very graceful while that of the other is stiffer, you can remember this for future reference more easily if you know that graceful flyer is a Cabbage White. And, of course, if you want to communicate your experiences with other butterfly enthusiasts, names are quite important.

HOW TO IDENTIFY BUTTERFLIES

The first step in identifying a butterfly is to realize that you are viewing a butterfly. One of the most common questions asked about butterflies is, "What's the difference between a moth and a butterfly?" Before answering this, let's look at where butterflies

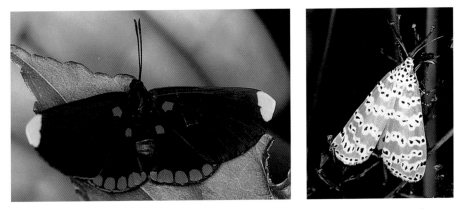

Compare the antennas on this Red-bordered Pixie *(left)*, a type of metalmark found in the Lower Rio Grande Valley of Texas, with those of the bella moth *(right)*.

fit in the overall scheme of living animals. Butterflies and moths belong with the vast army of animals that lack a backbone — invertebrates.

Within this group are the insects, the most numerous class of animals on the earth. The insect class is broken up into different "orders" — beetles, dragonflies and damselflies, flies, etc. One of these orders is the lepidoptera — moths and butterflies. The word "lepidoptera" means scaly-winged, and these scales are characteristic of moths and butterflies.

Scientists have further divided the lepidoptera into groups of related species. One of these groups is the group we call butterflies. All the other groups we call moths. There are more than 100,000 moth species.

So, how can we tell a butterfly from a moth? Well, scientists use a welter of technical characteristics that distinguish the butterflies quite well but would be difficult for the average person to apply. I will point out a few generalities that work most of the time. First, almost all adult butterflies fly during the daytime. In contrast, the vast majority of moths are nocturnal, that is, they fly at night. But, there are still many moths that fly during the day.

Second, most moths have a structure, called the frenulum, that hooks the forewing to the hindwing. This results in a flight pattern that is stiff and herky-jerky. Butterflies lack a frenulum and thus, in general, fly much more gracefully than most moths.

Lastly, look carefully at the antennas. Butterfly antennas look something like a golf club, with a long shaft and a club at the end. In contrast, moth antennas come in two basic varieties. Either the moth's antennas are simple filaments, tapering to a point, or they are complex with crossbars, like TV antennas. In addition, if your lepidopteran does not fit into any of the families shown in this book, it is probably a moth.

But, as you gain experience looking at butterflies, you will find that you won't need to rely on any of these characteristics. You will soon recognize a butterfly by its overall "feel."

The next step in identification is to place the butterfly into one of the six families found in the United States. *Notice the size of the butterfly.* Swallowtails are large, whites and yellows are medium-sized, and gossamer-wings are small. *Notice the color of the butterfly.* Blues, a subfamily of gossamer-wings, are generally blue, whites and yellows are white or yellow, and brushfoots or usually orange-brown. *Notice the wing shape.* Grass-skippers have narrow, angular wings while gossamer-wings have squarer, more rounded wings. *Notice the flight pattern.* Hairstreaks fly in a rapid and circular pattern, satyrs bounce over the vegetation with an undulating flight, while grass-skippers streak over the grass tops.

Swallowtails: How do you recognize a swallowtail? Ask the butterfly three questions: "Are you large?" "Are you not orange?" and "Are you tailed?" Most butterflies are small to medium-sized, while swallowtails are large. Most of the non-swallowtails that are large, such as greater fritillaries and monarchs, are orange-colored. Although a few non-swallowtails, such as Mourning Cloak and the admirals, are large, no other large butterflies have tails. The only wrinkle here are the parnassians: swallowtails that are large and white and without tails.

Whites and Yellows: Almost all members of this family actually are either white or yellow, making their family identification easy. And to make things even easier, the whites are generally white and the yellows are generally yellow or orange. The whites and yellows can sometimes be exasperatingly difficult to see well, because of their tendency to keep moving. Even while nectaring, many species stay at a particular flower for only a short time.

Gossamer-wings: With few exceptions, these are small, delicate butterflies with wing shapes that are very different from other small butterflies such as skippers.

Within the gossamer-wings, some subgroups are soon recognizable. Blues are mostly blue above. If you call all small butterflies with blue topsides "blues," you will not be misidentifying many butterflies. Hairstreaks are often tailed. Again, if you call all small butterflies with tails hairstreaks, you'll almost always be right (the only exclusions are tailed-blues and Tailed Copper, both illustrated in this book).

Metalmarks: This exciting group of New World butterflies is the most diverse of any family. Although most of these species are similar to one another, in the tropics there is an amazing variety of sizes, colors, patterns, and wing shapes. Most similar to the gossamer-wings, almost all of these species can be recognized as metalmarks by noticing their green eyes.

Brushfoots: So-called because males have their front two legs reduced to small stubs, or "brushes." This is the most difficult group to characterize, but contains many of our best-known butterflies. Monarchs and Mourning Cloaks are brushfoots, as are Viceroys and Painted Ladies. Most species' wings are colored a combination of brownish orange and black. Perhaps the easiest way to recognize a butterfly as a brushfoot is to realize that it's not a swallowtail, white or yellow, gossamer-wing, metalmark, or skipper. Actually, this isn't hard to do.

Some brushfoot subgroups are easier to recognize than are others. For example, satyrs are mainly medium-sized and brown, with a characteristic bobbing flight.

Skippers: Some butterfliers ignore the skippers altogether. But I would argue that to do so deprives you of some great pleasures (see the photos of beamers, for example). Realistically, however, I must admit that identifying members of this family can be frustrating, mainly because so many of the species are small and so closely resemble one another. All that being said, I think that you have a good chance of placing most of the skippers you see into one of the groups described in this book.

In general, skippers are easy to place to subfamily. You can ignore the one firetip subfamily skipper in the United States (found only in extreme southeastern Arizona, and not illustrated in this book) and there are only a few skipperlings, most of which are uncommon and narrowly distributed. Giant-skippers are wonderful, but for a variety of reasons they are rarely seen. Thus, any skipper you see is likely to be either a spread-wing skipper or a grass-skipper. These are easy to distinguish. Spread-wing skippers are larger than grass-skippers and have a different wing shape. Grass-skippers have angular, long wings, while spread-wing skippers' wings are rounder and not as narrow. In addition, spread-wing skippers open their forewings and hindwings in unison; grass-skippers uniquely hold their forewings and hindwings at a different angle from each other. When the wings are fully opened, the hindwings are held flat while the forewings are held at an acute angle, giving them something of a jet-plane appearance. No other butterflies look like this.

Now that you've established what family your butterfly belongs to, you might want to try to identify it to one of the groups shown in this book. To do that it helps to know what side of the butterfly you're looking at — its topside or its underside. Occasionally this can be a bit more confusing than you would think. Most often the topside and underside of the same butterfly are very different (see the illustrations of Mexican Bluewing on this page).

Also, keep in mind that males and females of most butterfly species differ in appearance. With many species this is quite subtle — female tiger swallowtails have more blue along the hindwing border than do males — but for some species the differences are dramatic. Male Diana Fritillaries are orange while females are dark blue. Little Yellow males are bright yellow while a fair number of females are white.

The topside and underside of the same butterfly can be dramatically different. A Mexican Bluewing has brilliant blue stripes *(left)*, but is camouflaged against tree bark when its wings are closed *(right)*.

Male and female butterflies of the same species often look different. ***Top:*** Male Little Yellows are yellow, while some of the females are white. ***Bottom, left and right:*** Male Zabulon Skippers are bright yellow while females are dark brown with a different pattern.

Butterfly Biology

LIFE CYCLE

The Mourning Cloak that you startle as you round a bend on the woodlands road; the large, black-striped, bright yellow tiger swallowtail that excites your whole family as they watch it nectaring at your lilacs; the stately Monarchs that you watch with awe as they sail south in the fall, headed for their winter home in the Mexican mountains — none of these adult butterflies would appear for your enjoyment without the presence of their immature stages.

Each butterfly goes through four distinct stages in its life. Egg, caterpillar, pupa, and adult. Let's start with a female adult butterfly and follow the next generation.

Eggs

Assuming that the adult female butterfly has mated (and almost all do), she will be carrying fertilized eggs. She will spend a considerable part of her day searching for an appropriate plant on which to lay her eggs. An appropriate plant is one that the newly hatched caterpillar is able to use as food. Later, we will learn more about caterpillar foodplants.

There is much to enjoy about eggs, especially if you have a magnifying lens that allows you to see them better. The size, shape, and color of eggs vary from species to species, and most dramatically among the various families of butterflies. Many eggs have a beautiful and intricate architecture.

How and where the female places the eggs are also interesting. Some species lay only one egg per plant. Others place a mass of eggs together. Some species lay their eggs mainly on flower buds, others place them on the undersides of leaves, while still others lay their eggs at the base of a tree. How many eggs a particular female lays varies greatly from species to species. Over the course of their lives, some butterflies lay only a few dozen eggs, most probably lay a few hundred, and some, such as the Regal Fritillary, lay a few thousand.

A Bordered Patch lays her mass of eggs on the underside of a leaf.

Butterflies employ a variety of egg-laying strategies. **Clockwise from top:** Viceroys lay their eggs at the tips of willow leaves. Empress Leilia eggs are strung like pearls. Monarchs often lay their eggs singly on a milkweed flower petal. Question Mark eggs are ribbed and stacked.

Caterpillars

When the egg hatches, usually after less than a week, a tiny caterpillar emerges. This voracious eating machine spends almost all its time eating and growing. As it rapidly increases in size, it outgrows its outer skin (called an exoskeleton). The old skin splits and is shed, revealing a new, larger and baggier skin below. This process happens a number of times (usually four or five) over the course of about two or three weeks. Each stage between skin shedding is termed an instar. At different stages in its development, the caterpillar can appear dramatically different. For example, last-instar caterpillars of Guava Skippers are milky white, while the penultimate-instar caterpillars are brilliant red with cream bands (see p. 19). Caterpillars of related species often look different but have similarities. Zebra Heliconian caterpillars are white with black dots while Gulf Fritillaries are orange with black dots. But they both have similar black spines.

Caterpillars have various defense mechanisms. Some roll themselves into balls at the first sign of trouble, other take the offensive. Many swallowtail caterpillars extrude

Closely related species, such as the Zebra Heliconian caterpillars *(above)* and the Gulf Fritillary caterpillar *(left)*, have obvious differences but share some similarities.

There can be more than one color form of the same type of caterpillar. Both of the photos above are of Cloudless Sulphur caterpillars.

special structures, termed osmeteria, that they normally keep concealed (see Giant Swallowtail caterpillar photo on page 59). These release a foul-smelling aroma intended to fend off predators. Some swallowtails, such as Spicebush Swallowtail, have false eye-spots on their heads, making them look like snakes or flamboyant mini-dragons. Others that contain toxic chemicals sport bright colors and patterns as if to say "Back off—I don't taste very good."

Many skipper caterpillars, and others, roll themselves up in leaves, so that they are not easily visible. Others, such as Silver-banded Hairstreak, develop inside a seed pod, hidden from most of the world and would-be diners. However, most caterpillars protect themselves by blending in with their surroundings.

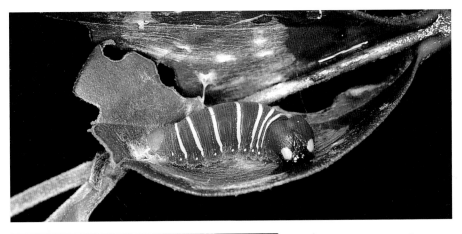

Guava Skipper caterpillars change radically from the penultimate instar *(above)* to the last instar *(left)*.

Below: Some caterpillars, such as this black-phase Pipevine Swallowtail caterpillar (see page 53 for an illustration of the red phase), often wander around out in the open. Their strong colors and pattern serve to alert would-be predators to the presence of toxic chemicals.

Some caterpillars defend against predation by living in a protected environment. A balloon vine *(above)* attracts a female Silver-banded Hairstreak *(right)* which lays an egg on the surface of one of the seed pods (or "balloon"). The caterpillar *(below)* burrows into the pod and develops within it. Locate balloon vines and you may find Silver-banded Hairstreaks (on the Florida Keys and in extreme South Texas).

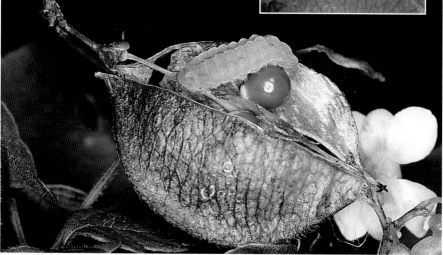

Pupas

When the caterpillar has grown to full size, it attaches itself to a support and pupates. Sometimes this happens on the caterpillar foodplant itself, but more often the caterpillar wanders away from the foodplant and attaches itself to a twig or a blade of grass. The caterpillar, now encased in a hard outer shell (the chrysalis), becomes a pupa — seemingly lifeless and inert. But inside the hard outer shell, an amazing transformation is taking place. The tissues and structures of the caterpillar are being broken down and replaced with the tissues and structures of the adult butterfly. If development is proceeding straight through, this process usually takes one to two weeks. Or the pupa may enter a resting state for a few months, or for the winter.

Adults

When the adult is fully formed, the chrysalis splits open and the adult butterfly emerges (ecloses). In the chrysalis, the wings are wrapped tightly around the butterfly's body. Upon emergence, fluid is pumped through the "veins" in the wings and they are unfurled. This is a very vulnerable time in a butterfly's life, as it basks in the sunshine to harden and set its wings. Once the adult butterfly emerges from the chrysalis it no longer grows larger. So, if you see a small butterfly flying around, it is not a baby butterfly! It is a fully formed adult.

Left: An Empress Leilia pupa blends with the leaf on which it rests.

Below: The bright red color of Atala pupas warn potential predators of toxic chemicals.

A Polydamas Swallowtail pupa hangs by a silk thread. It's general shape is characteristic of swallowtails.

Lifespan

When people ask the question "How long does a butterfly live?", they most commonly mean, "How long does an adult butterfly live?" The answer is: Some small blues may live less than a week, while large brushfoots, such as Mourning Cloaks and Monarchs, may live up to about nine months. The majority of adult butterflies usually live about two to four weeks, if they do not fall prey to predators.

Broods

As we've seen, the butterfly life cycle goes as follows: adult, egg, caterpillar, pupa, adult. Some species of butterflies go through this cycle only once per year. Over much of the northern part of its range, the Mourning Cloak fits this pattern. Adult butterflies spend the winter in shelters, such as hollows in trees. In the springtime they become active and the females lay eggs. The eggs hatch, the caterpillars eat and then pupate in early summer. About the end of June, the new adults emerge and begin a new cycle.

Most butterflies have more than one cycle, or brood, each year. Many species have a definite number of broods that fly at specific times of the year. For example in the northeastern United States, Juniper Hairstreak adults fly in April through May. The females lay eggs; caterpillars hatch, eat, and pupate; and new adults emerge and fly in July and August. The offspring of the July–August brood spend the winter in the pupal stage, then the adults emerge and fly the next April–May.

Some species are more or less continuously brooded throughout the year. Cabbage White is a good example. A succession of individuals of this species fly from the first warm weather in spring until hard frosts in the fall.

A newly emerged Dingy Purplewing clings to its chrysalis. Soon after emerging, butterflies expel the stored up excretory products of the pupa, which appears as a thick reddish fluid. Rare mass emergences of butterflies have given rise to tales of blood pouring from the sky.

STRUCTURES

The body of an adult butterfly is divided into three sections: the head; the middle of the body, called the thorax; and the abdomen.

The head has two eyes. These are quite different from our eyes in that each eye is composed of hundreds of subunits, each of which functions as an eye. Two antennas rise from the head and sensitive chemoreceptors — allowing a sense of smell — are located on the swellings or clubs near their far ends. The head also contains a mouth, through which a long, coiled, tube-like tongue emerges. The tongue functions like a drinking straw, enabling the butterfly to sip fluids such as nectar from flowers or moisture from damp sand.

Forewing

Antenna

Hindwing

Tongue

A Dorcas Copper nectars at its caterpillar food plant, shrubby cinquefoil.

The thorax contains internal organs and has two pairs of wings and three pairs of legs attached to it. The set of wings closest to the head are the forewings, while the rear pair are the hindwings. The wings contain thickened veins that serve as struts to support the wings, and through which fluid is pumped to expand the wings when the adult emerges from its chrysalis. The wings themselves are covered with scales. Wing colors result from pigments on the scales and/or from the structure of the scales themselves. All iridescence is structural as are most blue colors. Greens usually are created by a combination of blue and yellow.

The abdomen contains, among other organs, the butterfly's sexual organs. When butterflies mate, the male and female join at the ends of their abdomens, facing back-to-back.

A Desert Orangetip displays its topside.

BEHAVIOR

Basking

Butterflies are cold-blooded — their body temperature largely depends on the ambient temperature. Thus, when it is cold outside, butterflies want to warm up and can employ two different basking strategies to do so. Some butterflies sit in the sunshine in an exposed spot (or even better, on a warm rock) and open their wings. This allows the sun's rays to warm them. Some spring and cold-climate flying white butterflies are especially adapted to this type of dorsal basking. They open their white wings part way and sit in the sunshine. The sun's rays bounce off the angled white wings and are directed to the black body, where the warmth does the most good.

Other butterflies use lateral basking. These butterflies, including many of our spring hairstreaks, sit in the sunshine with their wings closed. Then they tilt their bodies so that the plane of their wings is perpendicular to the sun's rays, thus most efficiently capturing the warming energy of the sun.

Courtship

Like humans, different butterflies have different courting styles and strategies. Males of some species choose a territory — maybe the spot is at the top of the hill or, to his eye, has a particularly fine perch. In the event, the male hangs out in his territory waiting for a female to fly by. While he's waiting, he's likely to try to chase off other males of his species. Actually, he probably will chase after all other butterflies, or anything that moves for that matter, including people.

A Coronis Fritillary basks in the early morning sun to warm up at high altitude in Great Basin National Park in Nevada.

Other males take a more proactive approach. One might keep on flying till he finds a female, for instance. This patrolling behavior works for him, but can be annoying to the butterflier who wants to snap his photo. Males of some species can adopt either the perching or the patrolling behavior, depending upon environmental conditions such as population density.

Actual courtship can be fairly elaborate or virtually nonexistent. Some males simply fly up to a female, land sideways on her wings, and immediately mate. Others try wafting attractive perfumes (pheromones) over the female to entice her. Some species

Above left: Butterfly courtships sometimes degenerate into a ménage à trois, this one involving a female Falcate Orangetip at the center and two pursuing males. ***Above right:*** Other males take a more subtle approach. Here a male Barred Yellow has opened his right forewing and placed it in front of the object of his ardor. Depending upon the impressiveness of his black bar and the sweetness of the perfume that emanates from it, the female will decide whether he is a desirable match.

have little mating dances, with synchronized movements. But, relatively little is known about most species' courtship behavior; perhaps the best way to add to your knowledge is by close observation.

You can almost always tell if a female is rejecting a male (which most females do most of the time). If the female is sticking her abdomen into the air she is saying "Forget about it." If she is rapidly vibrating her wings she is saying "I'd rather waste all this energy than get close to you."

Hilltopping

Many humans go to singles bars because prospective mates may be concentrated at these locations. Hilltops are the butterfly equivalent of singles bars. The males of many butterfly species may be most easily found by climbing to the top of the highest hill in the vicinity, especially if the top of the hill is open and if at least some of the slopes are quite steep. Here, the males patrol the area looking for females. Unmated females also fly up here (otherwise the system wouldn't work), but already mated females spend more time elsewhere, looking for caterpillar foodplants and nectar.

Gully Bottoming

This is the upside-down version of hilltopping. Just as humans with different mating predilections may frequent specialized singles bars, some butterflies choose to mate at the lowest point around. Even within gullies, there will be specialization, so that if you check the edges of the gully and then check the center, you may well find different species.

Learning

Although they may not qualify as geniuses, butterflies are capable of learning. Given their intimate involvement with flowers, it is not surprising that laboratory experiments have shown that they can learn to recognize colors that will lead to a nectar reward. Species that live the longest, for example heliconians, clearly learn the locations of the important nectar sources in their neighborhood, often flying a particular route each day. Although there is no real evidence that butterflies communicate with one another, as bees do, I have found, for example, fifty Acadian Hairstreaks at dogbane flowers located about one-half mile from where the hairstreaks emerged as adults, in a field blocked by trees from the birth site. Did each of these hairstreaks find these flowers on its own?

Mudpuddling and Nutrient Recycling

Although butterflies are viewed by many as ethereal creatures, they often get down and dirty. Some of the best places to find butterflies are at the edges of mudpuddles or at damp sand. In general, these are stag parties, with only males in attendance (although the females of some species do come to mudpuddles). The butterflies aren't normally there to drink water, they are obtaining salts that are dissolved in the mineral-laden water. The males especially need these salts, because during mating they transfer huge amounts of salts to help provide nutrients for eggs. If you closely observe these puddle parties, you'll notice that very often individuals segregate out by species. That is, individuals of the same species clump together. Watch some more, and you'll see that the butterflies are watching each other! When one individual finds a particularly choice and salty spot, other individuals of the same species will soon come to the exact, and I mean exact, same spot.

Another place at which butterflies sometimes aggregate is at flowing sap, on rotting fruit, or at animal scat. Here, there are proteins and other nutrients that can't be found in nectar. The butterflies aren't too concerned with where these nutrients have been, they just instinctively know that they will increase their longevity and give them a greater chance of passing along their genes to the next generation.

PARASITES AND DISEASES

Very few (perhaps one or two out of 100) butterflies survive the journey from egg to adult. Most are killed by parasites and diseases. Many parasitic wasps lay their eggs on butterfly caterpillars. These are probably the single biggest butterfly killers. In addition, caterpillars are very susceptible to infection by fungi, bacteria, and viruses. And for many species, there is a fine line between conditions that are too dry, which can cause

Top: A group of tiger swallowtails gains nourishment from animal scat. *Bottom:* A Tawny Emperor investigates a tree-rottened orange.

the caterpillars to die of dessication, and those that are too wet, which promote the growth of death-inducing fungi.

PREDATORS

While butterflies have friends, they have enemies too. Lots of animals like to eat butterflies or their caterpillars. Birds, lizards, praying mantises, and spiders are just a few of the creatures lurking in the shadows wanting to make a meal of an unsuspecting butterfly. Crab spiders, colored to match the color of the flower on which they wait, often succeed. Butterflies employ a variety of strategies to avoid becoming a meal.

Cryptic Coloration

Many butterflies have wing patterns that blend in with their surroundings. Leafwings, a largely tropical group, one of which occurs commonly throughout the southeastern United States, actually do look remarkably like leaves. Other species have wing patterns that are disruptive, making it difficult for a predator to recognize them as butterflies.

Even while mating, a mantis can't resist fast food, in this case a hapless Ocola Skipper.

Many butterflies fall prey to spiders. Especially busy are crab spiders, such as this one **(above)**, which has captured a Dorcas Copper. Other types of spiders, including the orb weaver and the jumping spider **(left)**, also feast on butterflies. In this case the jumping spider's victim is a Many-spotted Skipperling, a species rarely seen in the United States.

Mimicry

Some butterflies mimic the appearance of other butterflies. They do this because some butterfly species contain various toxic chemicals that make them unpalatable to birds. If a palatable species looks just like the unpalatable species, birds may not eat either. The classic case of this type of mimicry is the palatable Viceroy mimicking the unpalatable Monarch. Recently, it has been found that, at least in some parts of the country, the Viceroy itself is actually unpalatable.

Why would two or more species that each are unpalatable mimic each other? Well, the theory is that the more bad-tasting butterflies that a bird encounters, the faster that bird will learn to avoid other butterflies that look similar.

False Heads

Some butterflies, especially the hairstreaks, have a pattern on their underwings that creates the appearance of a head at the tail end of the butterfly. A pattern of lines draws attention to the posterior, where a spot near the corner of the hindwing looks like an eye (especially because the wing is flared outward at this spot) and where the tails of the hairstreak look like antennas. When the butterfly moves its hindwings back and forth, making the fake antennas move, the deception is complete.

When a bird or other predator sees the hairstreak, it often attacks the tail end, thinking that it is the head. The predator comes away with a piece of the wing, while the hairstreak flies away. The next time you see some hairstreaks, watch them to see if they "saw" their hindwings back and forth.

Myrmecophily

This great scrabble word means ant-loving. The caterpillars of some butterflies, especially of the gossamer-wings and metalmarks, closely associate with ants. These caterpillars are equipped with special glands that secrete a sweet "honey-dew" substance. Many ants, being very fond of sweets, tend the caterpillars so that they (the ants) can eat this substance. Thus, the ants protect the caterpillars from less friendly ants and

The hindwings of many hairstreaks have tails and a black spot near the tail. To many a predator, the tails appear to be antennas while the black spot appears to be an eye. The subterfuge is further enhanced when the hairstreak "saws" its wings back and forth, making its false antennas wave in the air. Predators will often attack the false head, allowing the hairstreak to escape with just some of its wings missing.

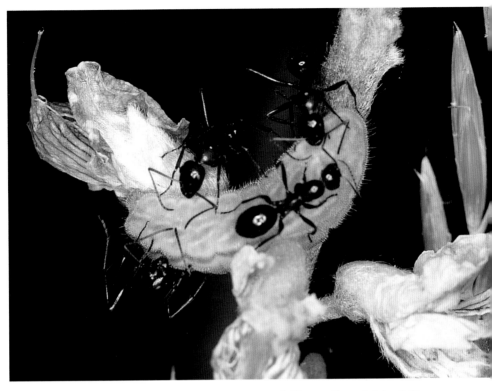

Caterpillars of some species of butterflies almost always are tended by ants. Here a Boisduval's Blue caterpillar gets the full treatment at the ant spa, massage included.

from other predators. Sometimes the caterpillars spend a lot of time in the ant nest themselves. And the caterpillars of some species of blues found in other parts of the world actually turn on their ant protectors and eat them. Some of the ants and caterpillars are so closely connected that the distribution of the butterfly species is limited by the distribution of particular ant species.

Overnighting and Overwintering

When nighttime comes or the weather is inclement, butterflies seek shelter. The type of shelter may vary depending upon the habitat in which the butterfly lives. Many butterflies that live in meadows crawl down into the tight root masses of the grasses. Woodland butterflies may spend the night on the underside of a tree leaf. Arctics, living in rocky alpine habitats, often crawl into rock crevices. Most butterflies spend the night singly, but some species, such as Zebra Heliconians, often form communal roosts.

In northern climes, winter is a difficult time for butterflies. Yet butterflies survive even in the frigid arctic. They do this by spending the winter in a sort of suspended animation, called diapause, where their bodily functions slow to near zero. The great majority of butterfly species spend the winter as either caterpillars or as pupas. A few overwinter as eggs. Among the butterflies included here, only the anglewings and the tortoiseshells (which are closely related to each other) and Goatweed Leafwing normally spend the winter in the north as adult butterflies. Sheltered in tree holes or crevices, or in crevices in man-made structures, commas or Mourning Cloaks can be seen flying about on warm sunny days, even in the dead of winter.

Traveling Butterflies

Most butterflies live and die close to the spot where they were born. But butterflies have wings and are capable of traveling long distances. Some adult butterflies fly away from the area in which they were born. These individuals radiate out, presumably in random directions, searching for new suitable home sites. So although many butterflies are normally very habitat-restricted — for example Hessel's Hairstreak is normally found only in white cedar swamps — it is possible to find a traveling butterfly out of habitat.

When people talk about "migration" they usually mean a northward movement in the spring followed by a southward movement in the fall. Many butterflies that spend the summer in the northern half of the United States cannot survive northern winters. Each year, as the weather becomes warmer, butterflies from the southern United States and Mexico fly north to repopulate these regions. Species that move northward each year include Cloudless Sulphur, Little Yellow, Marine Blue, Painted Lady, Red Admiral, Clouded Skipper, Sachem, and Fiery Skipper. In especially good years, one can see Cloudless Sulphurs and Painted Ladies streaming northward out of Mexico.

The movement south, in the fall, is usually far less obvious for these species. But for another group of species, the fall migration is more obvious. Each fall, Question Marks, Mourning Cloaks, Common Buckeyes, Monarchs, and Queens fly southward in variable, but sometimes very impressive, concentrations. On one September day I observed about six thousand Monarchs, four thousand Red Admirals, four thousand Question Marks, and two thousand Mourning Cloaks flying south through a ten-foot-wide path adjacent to a beach in New York City.

We don't really know if the Red Admirals, Question Marks, and Mourning Cloaks concentrate in certain areas for the winter. In fact, we know very little about the details of most butterfly movements. But we do have quite a bit of information about Monarchs.

Monarch Migration

Most of the adult North American Monarchs east of the Continental Divide fly southward in the fall. Many of them follow natural features, such as coastlines, river valleys, and mountain ridges. Some follow unnatural features and can be seen sailing high above New York City's traffic-clogged skyscraper canyons. The Monarchs often form impressive congregations at favored resting stops along the way, including Point Pelee in Ontario, the barrier beaches of Long Island, the Cape May Peninsula in New Jersey, and at various sites in central and south Texas, including Eagle Pass. Exactly where, when, and how large these masses will be depends upon each year's environmental conditions.

These migrating Monarchs eventually make their way to the Transvolcanic Range of central Mexico. There, high in the fir-clad mountains, at altitudes of more than 10,000 feet, perhaps 100 million of these orange and black butterflies blanket the trees, color the sky, and create one of the truly great spectacles of the natural world.

Millions of Monarchs turn fir trees orange and weigh down their boughs in mountains above Angangueo, Michoacan, Mexico.

In the spring, Monarchs fly north. Only a few, perhaps one in a million, make it back to the northern United States. The rest lay eggs on milkweeds in northern Mexico and in the southern United States. Their offspring then finish the migration north.

West of the Rocky Mountains, most Monarchs fly the relatively short distance to the central California coast where they spend the winter in large communal roosts. The city of Pacific Grove has given the overwintering roost sites protected status.

Butterfly Gardening

A rapidly growing number of people are combining the satisfaction that comes from gardening with the excitement and drama that butterflies provide. How widespread is butterfly gardening? One recent October day I was at Santa Ana National Wildlife Refuge in Alamo, Texas. The refuge, long famous for birds and becoming equally famous for butterflies, had created a butterfly garden in front of the headquarters building. That day, the garden was filled with a kaleidoscope of butterflies — perhaps sixty species — and with butterfliers from around the country. A family group of non-butterfliers approached the garden on their way into the refuge. The father, seeing the amazing activity at the garden, exclaimed, "Wow, look at all those butterflies over there!" The son, who was perhaps six years old, replied, "Of course, Dad, that's a butterfly garden."

So how do you actually create a butterfly garden? Plant some pretty flowers? Plant flowers that attract butterflies? Well, yes, in part. But if you want to create a truly successful butterfly garden, you need to provide the plants that caterpillars eat. Remember, without caterpillars there are no adult butterflies.

Choosing flowers is the easy part because there are so many at which butterflies love to nectar. And because very few species of butterflies have particular likes when

A butterfly garden, such as this one in southeastern Arizona, can be attractive both to butterflies and humans.

Asters are dual-purpose butterfly garden plants — crescent caterpillars use asters as foodplants while the flowers provide nectar to adult butterflies in the fall, when nectar sources are scarce.

it comes to flowers, there are many flowers you can choose that will be attractive to a broad array of butterfly species, even those from different families. But caterpillars are more persnickety! Some eat only a single group of related plants, while others eat only one particular plant species. For example, Fulvia Checkerspot caterpillars will eat only Indian paintbrushes, but they will eat a number of different species of the plant, while Harris' Checkerspot caterpillars will eat only flat-topped white aster.

Because caterpillars are so particular, the plants that are useful in a butterfly garden will vary tremendously from place to place, depending upon the species of butterflies nearby. One's selection of plants also will be influenced by local populations. For example, butterflies learn the common nectar sources in their environment and they have a predilection toward nectaring at flowers they are already familiar with. So, using native nectar sources that are common in the vicinity of your garden is a good idea. In addition, butterflies like flowers with lots of nectar, and how much nectar a particular flower has often depends upon its growing conditions. The performance of the same species of plant as a butterfly garden plant may vary depending upon local soil, sun, and climate conditions. Even the time of day will affect a plant's nectar output and thus its attractiveness to butterflies.

What is the practical importance of all this to the would-be butterfly gardener? It is that in addition to continent-wide information, one needs site-specific information and experience. The broad picture I paint here should be supplemented with local color and detail. Where can you find this local information? Ultimately, the best sources will be the butterfly gardening brochures at the North American Butterfly Association's website (www.naba.org) and from local NABA chapters. Even with all available information at hand, the best procedure is to actually test various plants in your garden to see how well they do. General suggestions for groups of plants suitable for butterfly gardening are listed in this section. Many other suggestions are made throughout this

Above left: Buckwheats are beautiful, primarily western, garden plants that provide nectar and are used by many caterpillars as well. ***Above right:*** Milkweeds provide food for Monarch caterpillars and for many adult butterflies.

book in the Gardening Suggestion section of each group account. Part of the fun is experimentation. Of course, actually getting to see those caterpillars grow in your garden is pretty exciting also!

Although the list of plants that are potentially useful for a butterfly garden is truly extensive, some groups of plants top the list as must-haves for most parts of the United States. Very high on the list are the milkweeds. Not only are milkweeds the required caterpillar foodplants for Monarchs and their relatives, they are important native nectar sources — and beautiful to boot! See pages 40 and 41 for illustrations and descriptions of a selection of milkweeds. Asters are another useful group that serves two functions: they are the caterpillar foodplants for a number of crescents and are very useful fall nectar sources.

In the West, every butterfly garden should have buckwheats, sensational plants that succor caterpillars and adults of many butterfly species. In the eastern two-thirds of the country, if you have the space, seriously consider planting a hackberry tree. Caterpillars of three species of emperors (two of them widespread and relatively common) as well as American Snout and Question Mark all use these trees for food. Plus, their nuts are used by other wildlife (just because you're focused on butterflies doesn't mean that you have to ignore other animals). In southern climes, passion vines and sennas are de rigueur if you want heliconians and yellows in your garden.

For nectar, you have a broad array of possibilities. Try, of course, to have a variety of plants that will provide nectar throughout the butterfly season, taking into account the bloom seasons of individual plants. One plant that is particularly attractive to

Top left: Violets are the only caterpillar foodplants for greater fritillares. **Top right:** Passion vines are a must-have plant for the southern butterfly garden, attracting widespread and dazzling Gulf Fritillaries. **Bottom:** Ceanothus, sometimes called California lilacs, provide food for caterpillars and adults.

almost all butterflies, and that works over most of the United States, is butterfly bush. Most butterfly gardens outside of the hottest areas include this non-native plant, but there is growing concern that it may become invasive and a problem. At least in the Northeast, there are a few areas where this alien is now naturalized, forming dense thickets along highway borders.

Plants that are widely available through local nurseries are attractive for a number of reasons: they are easy to obtain, have been bred to grow easily in gardens, and are more consistent than are wild plants. But, ultimately, using plants that are native to your local area will usually prove to be more effective for the butterflies, and more satisfying to you.

Another suggestion is to mass nectar sources and caterpillar foodplants, as groups of plants are more attractive than a few individual plants would be.

As mentioned earlier, milkweeds are great butterfly gardening plants. There are scores of species of milkweeds in the United States. Most are used to some extent by

Purple milkweed.

Monarch and Queen caterpillars. Many are also excellent nectar plants, providing sustenance for large numbers of butterflies of many species. Some outstanding species for the butterfly garden are shown on these pages. Throughout much of the eastern two-thirds of the country, swamp milkweed and orange milkweed are consistent performers. Swamp milkweed usually is much showier than the example shown on the opposite page and, despite its name, will do just fine in ordinary garden soil. Mexican milkweed is an excellent choice for areas without freezes or as an annual farther north. In the Rocky Mountains and Pacific Northwest, showy milkweed is a widespread species. On the Pacific Coast, narrow-leaved milkweed is a native worth trying.

Many milkweeds contain chemicals that are poisonous to animals. Some milkweeds, such as orange milkweed, are less toxic than are others. Monarch caterpillars, eating the toxic plants, accumulate these chemicals and thus become distasteful to potential predators. Because eating milkweeds can adversely affect livestock, in some areas it is illegal to plant milkweeds. Despite the public uproar about BT corn (a genetically modified strain) and its potential effect on Monarchs, it is likely that bans on planting milkweeds, along with programs that attempt to destroy roadside milkweeds (and other plants) in the Midwest, directly affect Monarch populations much more seriously than BT corn possibly could.

In addition to providing caterpillar foodplants and adult nectar sources, you should consider providing windbreaks to shelter butterflies, flat stones on which butterflies can bask and warm up, and damp sand or gravel from which they can obtain salts. Fermenting fruit is also welcome, especially to many of the brushfoots. Keep in mind, however, that rotting fruit sometimes attracts other, unwanted insects, such as wasps, in addition to butterflies.

Having worked hard to create a butterfly garden, you should avoid the use of pesticides — they will kill your caterpillars and butterflies. Also, although many gardeners

Top: Mexican milkweed. ***Bottom left:*** A Monarch caterpillar eating swamp milkweed. ***Bottom right:*** Whorled milkweed.

Recommended Butterfly Garden Plants

Plant Name	Flowers Attractive to Adults	Caterpillar Foodplant for These Species
Alfalfa	YES	Orange Sulphur, Clouded Sulphur
Asters	YES	Pearl Crescent, Northern Crescent, Field Crescent
Blazing-stars	YES	none
Buckwheats (West)	YES	some blues, Mormon Metalmark
Butterfly bush	YES	none
Ceanothus	YES	California Tortoiseshell, some duskywings
Clovers, red & white	YES	Orange Sulphur, Clouded Sulphur, Eastern Tailed-Blue
Coneflowers	YES	none
Dandelions	YES	none
Deerweed (West)	YES	Orange Sulphur, Bramble Hairstreak, Marine Blue Anise
Fennel	NO	Swallowtail, Black Swallowtail
Fogfruits (South)	YES	Phaon Crescent, Common Buckeye, White Peacock
Goldenrods	YES	none
Hackberry trees	NO	American Snout, Question Mark, emperors
Heliotrope	YES	none
Kidneywood (South)	YES	Southern Dogface
Lantanas (South)	YES	Lantana Scrub-Hairstreak
Lupines	NO	Boisduval's Blue, Melissa Blue, Silvery Blue
Mallows	YES	Gray Hairstreak, Mallow Scrub-Hairstreak, Painted Lady, West Coast Lady, checkered-skippers
Mexican sunflower	YES	none
Milkweeds	YES	Monarch, Queen
Mistflowers	YES	some scintillant metalmarks
Passion vines (South)	NO	Gulf Fritillary, heliconians, Variegated Fritillary
Penta (South)	YES	none
Pipevines	NO	Pipevine Swallowtail
Rabbitbrush (West)	YES	none
Rock cresses (North)	YES	Marbles and orangetips
Sennas (South)	NO	Little Yellow, Sleepy Orange, Cloudless Sulphur, Orange-barred Sulphur
Sunflowers	YES	Bordered Patch, checkerspots
Thyme	YES	none
Verbenas (South)	YES	none
Violets (North and West)	SOMEWHAT	greater fritillaries
Wild black cherry (East)	SOMEWHAT	Eastern Tiger Swallowtail, Coral Hairstreak, Spring Azure, Red-spotted Purple
Willows (shrubs)	SOMEWHAT	Sylvan Hairstreak, Mourning Cloak, Viceroy, Lorquin's Admiral
Zinnias	YES	none

Butterfly bushes live up to the promise of their name. A wide array of butterflies, from large swallowtails to tiny skippers, all love to nectar at the fragrant blossoms of this garden plant. Although available in a variety of colors, including white and yellow, the standard blue-purple varieties seem to have the edge as butterfly attractors. **Above:** A butterfly bush paired with black-eyed Susans makes an attractive combination. **Left:** A butterfly bush attracts a worn male Eastern Tiger Swallowtail looking for an energy boost.

prefer a very neat look, butterflies do not. A little disorganization, allowing the presence of some weedy areas that will provide adventitous nectar sources and caterpillar food-plants, will create more butterflies that will then frequent your more formal garden.

Photography

Amazingly, photographing butterflies doesn't require any knowledge of photography at all. What you need is knowledge of butterflies and the right photographic equipment. The knowledge takes a little time to develop, and hopefully the information in this book will be helpful, allowing you to find butterflies, to understand something about their behavior, and to know what type of butterflies they are. But the equipment you need can be assembled in a flash — if you can afford it. Here's what you need for high-quality photographs.

A 35-millimeter camera. You can take pictures of butterflies with other cameras, but you, and others who view your photographs, are not likely to be happy with the results.

A 100-millimeter macro lens. A macro lens is extremely useful because many butterflies are quite small. If you're only going to photograph Monarchs and swallowtails, then you may not need one. But if you want to capture the beauty of hairstreaks and blues, you need a macro lens. Many lenses that claim to be macro lenses, including all those that are "zoom" macro lenses, are not. With a true macro lens, at closest focus the image of the butterfly will be life-size on the film.

A flash unit. Butterflies do not usually sit still for a picture (but see below). Using only natural light one must use slow shutter speeds to allow in enough light to sufficiently expose the film. When your shutter is slow and the butterfly is fast, your photograph is an out-of-focus blur. Even when the butterfly stays still, using natural light makes it very difficult to get all parts of the butterfly in focus, and the butterfly is almost always poorly lit. Because of this, I strongly recommend using a flash unit to supplement natural light. You can use a flash mounted on top of the camera, even the pop-up flash that comes with the camera, but for the most consistent results my advice is to use a ring flash. Because the ring flash wraps around the end of your lens, it is always aimed correctly.

Photographing butterflies does require some patience because some butterflies are very active. But most of the time, if you continue to watch the same butterfly, it will stop long enough for you to photograph it. Or another individual of the same species will be more cooperative. Or if you come back at a different time of the day, the butterflies may be moving more slowly. So I am a great believer in photographing butterflies as one finds them. Except as indicated, all photographs in this book are by the author and, if they are of butterflies, are of wild, unmanipulated butterflies.

You may be surprised to know that many butterfly photographs that appear on calendars, in magazines, and in books are taken by first capturing the butterfly, then putting it in a freezer to make it completely inactive, then placing it on an attractive flower with a composed background. Because the butterfly is now almost lifeless, the photographer can use a tripod and slow shutter speeds, allowing great depth of field. Often, photographs obtained in this manner are deceptive because one would never see the butterfly on the flower used or in the position posed. In addition, netting butterflies always carries with it the risk of harming the butterfly. Knowledgeable people can almost always recognize fake photographs, and thus they become aesthetically undesirable, just as most people wouldn't particularly enjoy a book about birds illustrated with photographs of stuffed birds. So just say no to fake photos!

Conservation

When people learn that I am involved with butterflies, often the first thing they ask me is, "I always used to see butterflies when I was a kid — how come there aren't any around any more?" Part of the reason has to do with the way that people live their lives and view the world. When you were a child you were small, observant, close to the ground, and probably played outside in fields of flowers — butterflies were part of your world. Now, you're much larger than butterflies, may not pay much attention to the natural world, and probably don't spend so much of your time rolling in meadows! Many people — to their loss — "outgrow" butterflies, but the pain is felt by the butterflies. Because the other part of the reason why people don't see as many butterflies is that there are fewer butterflies than before, and this relates directly to people not caring.

Miami Blues (shown here and on page 46), a species of black-eyed blue formerly common throughout southern Florida, are now known to be found in only a single colony on the Florida Keys. Habitat destruction and pest-control chemicals are almost certainly responsible for its decline. NABA is working to save this and other species.

The major reason for the reduced numbers of butterflies is that their habitats are being destroyed. Each time a new housing development goes up, or a new parking lot is paved, the butterflies that had lived on these plots of land perish, along with all the other plants and animals that had lived there. Because most butterflies are small and do not need vast vistas to survive, we can do much to ameliorate the effect of human population growth on butterflies. Throughout much of the United States there is a basic design to suburbia, featuring a limited palette of non-native shrubs, flowers, and grasses (for instance, rhododendrons, roses, and lawn grasses). Although these gardens and lawns may look attractive to people, they might as well be artificial movie sets as far as butterflies are concerned. If more people landscaped using native plants that support butterflies, healthy populations of many species of butterflies could easily coexist with people.

A second factor responsible for the decline of butterfly populations is the use of pesticides. Especially worrisome in this regard is the broadcast spraying of toxic anti–gypsy moth and anti-mosquito chemicals onto our forests and homes, respectively. Both programs kill butterflies wholesale and are probably responsible for causing the endangered situation in which some butterfly species find themselves. Both programs are misguided, in that they will not attain their goals and cause more harm than good, not only to butterflies, but, in the case of the anti-mosquito sprays, to people as well.

Miami Blue.

Some might say, "Butterflies are okay, but why save them? Let's focus on people." For starters, failing butterfly populations are early warning indicators of the deterioration of the environment. And butterflies are significant actors on the ecological stage, serving as food for other animals and as pollinators of many plants. But the importance of butterflies goes beyond these functional roles, and includes the symbolic role that these creatures play for people. Preserving a healthy environment of course has a direct and positive effect upon future generations, but butterflies should be protected and cared for simply because they represent such qualities as beauty and freedom to so many people. By helping to communicate your passion for butterflies to others, you will thus be helping to improve the world in more ways than one.

Commercially Raised Butterflies

"Releasing" butterflies at weddings and other events is a growing fad. The word "releasing" doesn't describe these events correctly, however, because the commercial butterfly farmers who sell these butterflies first imprison them in tiny envelopes and boxes. Usually, when the unsuspecting bride dumps out the contents of the box, the butterflies simply tumble to the ground, unable to fly after their period of imprisonment. On the two occasions when I was present at such events, that is exactly what happened. So they're not so much released as dumped on the ground.

Once "released," butterflies often find themselves in an environment in which they will die — either because they are already sick and dying, or because it's the wrong time of year for them, or because there is no suitable habitat for them in the vicinity. But the truly shocking conclusion is that, for the sake of our native wild butterflies, we must hope that these farm butterflies die quickly. Raised under unnatural conditions, farmed butterflies provide fertile ground for the spread of the many diseases that affect butterflies. The practice of shipping such butterflies around the country and releasing them into unsuitable environments could very easily result in the decimation of entire populations of our native butterflies by spreading disease epidemics.

These farmed butterflies create other problems as well. Recent scientific studies have shown that mixing farmed organisms with wild populations lowered the genetic fitness of the wild populations. Two of the most widely used butterflies for these "releases" are Monarchs and Painted Ladies. Both of these species migrate. We really know very little about these migrations. Since, for example, we have absolutely no idea how the Monarchs find their overwintering sites in central Mexico, it is entirely possible (not likely, but possible) that interactions with farm-raised Monarchs could interfere with the ability of wild Monarchs to migrate properly. Another obvious consequence of selling butterflies is that this creates a commercial market for living creatures. Even in our material society, this is a repugnant notion. It could also lead to the widespread slaughter of native wild butterflies. When a single Monarch for a wedding is worth ten dollars, there is much incentive for people to gather up wild Monarchs from migrating or overwintering aggregations and sell them.

Given all of these terrible potential consequences, why do commercial breeders continue the practice of raising and selling butterflies? The commercial interests behind these assaults on our native butterflies say that none of the abovementioned risks has been "proven," just as cigarette manufacturers said for decades that it wasn't "proven" that cigarettes caused cancer. As we all know, the fact was that the cigarette manufacturers didn't care if cigarettes caused cancer or not, and in fact knew that it did. Their only real interest was in making money. The commercial butterfly farmers that encourage releasing farmed-raised butterflies into the environment are much the same. They know the facts — they just don't care.

In the 1890s, people thought it would be wonderful to have all the birds mentioned by Shakespeare living here in North America. As a result, European Starlings were released into Central Park, New York. Since then, these birds have caused billions of dollars in damage to crops and harmed native songbirds around the country. Yet, if someone had asked, in 1890, "Where's the proof that this will damage the environment?," nobody could have provided such proof. Now that we have a good idea about what can result from tampering with ecosystems in this way, we can avoid similar disasters in the future by discouraging commercial interests that put the pursuit of profit above the health of the environment.

Above: Gulf Fritillary. ***Opposite:*** Lustrous Copper.

Species Guide

$\mathcal{T}$he photographs and descriptions on the following pages are designed to enable you to identify almost any butterfly you see to one of the groups shown in each two-page treatment. The groups described in these treatments are not artificial constructs, rather each group is composed of very similar species that are more closely related to each other than they are to other butterflies.

The order in which the groups are presented follows the taxonomic order used by the North American Butterfly Association (NABA).

Names

The common names of individual butterfly species are the official names used by the NABA. Prior to the publication of the first NABA *Checklist and English Names of North American Butterflies* in 1995, the authors of books dealing with butterlies used whatever English names they preferred, often coining new names with each book. The resulting confusion has stunted interest in butterflies. The rapid adoption of the NABA list as a standard will make it easy for the public to use a variety of books and understand which butterflies the authors are referring to. However, a number of widespread older books using outdated names are still in print and, because butterflying is so new, a minority of recent authors, mainly those coming from the older collecting tradition, are still using idiosyncratic names.

Because of this, I have provided a list of the scientific names that correspond to the common names as an appendix. However, as with the common names, in the past there has been widespread disagreement about scientific names. Again, the names used here are the official NABA scientific names, and almost all new publications will be using them.

The group names used in this work, names such as parnassians and duskywings, are, by and large, standardly used names for these groups of closely related butterfly species. Some names, for example "checkered metalmarks," have been used before, but not widely. A few group names, such as "beamers," have never been used before (but are now needed for a group of immediately recognizable tropical skippers). In most instances the group name corresponds, either exactly or roughly, to a genus of butterflies (*genus* is the scientific word for a group of similar species that are more closely related to each other than they are to other groups, and the first word of the two-part scientific name is the genus to which the species belongs).

Headings

The headings used in this section and their meanings are as follows:

NO. OF SPECIES: The number given here is the number of species resident in the region that is covered by this book: the "Lower 48," that is, the lower forty-eight states of the continental United States. If two numbers are given, the numbers refer to the first and second group mentioned in the heading, respectively. For example, on pages 112 and 113, "Silvery" and *Plebejus* blues are treated. The number of species is given as 2 + 7. This means that there are two species of "Silvery" blues and seven species of *Plebejus* blues in the area covered.

LENGTH OF FOREWING: The length of the line following this heading is the average forewing length of the species treated on that page. Remember that you can view either the topside or the underside of a butterfly. If a butterfly is perched with its wings closed, then the length of one forewing will be apparent, but if the butterfly has its wings open and spread, then the total width seen will be more than two times the length of one forewing (because in addition to the length of each of the two forewings there is the width of the butterfly's body).

Similar to the situation described with No. of Species, if there are two Length of Forewing bars, one refers to the first group mentioned while the other bar refers to the second group mentioned. If there are two groups described on a two-page section but only one Length of Forewing bar, this means that the length shown applies to both groups.

HOW TO KNOW THEM: This section describes how to recognize a butterfly as belonging to the particular group being treated. Many of the groups are composed of species that are very similar to each other but quite dissimilar in appearance from other species. For example, all the tiger swallowtails are quite similar and no other butterflies really resemble them. Recognizing a species as belonging to one of these groups should be relatively easy. Other groups are composed of more varied species and/or are not so dissimilar in appearance from other species. Recognizing a species as belonging to one of these groups will be more difficult.

WHERE THEY LIVE: A very general description of the habitats in which you might find members of this group.

WHAT THE CATERPILLARS EAT: A short list of the major plants eaten by caterpillars of the group.

WHAT THE ADULTS EAT: Most adult butterflies imbibe nectar for sustenance, but some eat other substances.

GARDENING SUGGESTIONS: A rough idea of the likelihood of having these butterflies in your garden, along with possible plants you can grow in order to attract them.

ABUNDANCE: The abundance of even one species may vary dramatically from region to region, from year to year, or at different times of the same year. When considering the abundance of multiple species, an accurate description becomes even more problematic. However, since there are some generalities, I think that it is useful to give you information about whether the species in this group tend to be rare, abundant, or in-between, along with an idea about the time of year they fly.

ETC.: Thoughts that do not naturally fit into one of the above categories.

MAP: Shows the range of this group in the Lower 48. Depending upon the number of species in a group and the complexity of their ranges, the map may show the range of the group as a whole, it may show the ranges of species within the group, or it may show the range of the group by flight times. For example, the map for "black" swallowtails shows the range of the six species in this group, taken as a group, while the map for the tailed-blue group shows the range of each of the two species in that group and the range where both species are found. By looking at the map, you can discern that if you see a tailed-blue in most of the East it is almost certain to be an Eastern Tailed-Blue while in most of the West it is almost certain to be a Western Tailed-Blue.

Some range maps show areas with different number of "flights." The term refers to periods of time, usually about one month, during which the adults of a species are flying. For some species there is only one flight during the year, but for other species there are two or three times during the year when adult butterflies of that species are flying. Usually, the adults flying at different times of the year are different individuals. The number of flights mainly corresponds to the number of broods a species has in a particular area (see page 22 for a discussion of broods). However, for a minority of species, successive flights may also reflect an influx of immigrant adult butterflies from farther south.

Range maps that show the number of flights per year allow you to judge the length-of-flight period in your area. In areas shown as having one flight, the butterflies in that group will probably be seen for a period of roughly a month. In areas shown as having three flights, the butterflies in that group may be seen through much of the warmer months.

Pipevine-feeding Swallowtails No. of species: 2

LENGTH OF FOREWING: ━━━━━━━━━━━━

HOW TO KNOW THEM: Pipevine Swallowtails have brilliant iridescent blue hindwings, both on their topsides and underwings, and a single row of large orange spots below. Polydamas Swallowtails have a pale yellow band across both wings and bright red spots on their bodies. Both species are perpetual motion machines, beating their forewings almost continually, even while nectaring.

WHERE THEY LIVE: Gardens, edges of woodlands, open thorn scrub.

WHAT THE CATERPILLARS EAT: Pipevines.

WHAT THE ADULTS EAT: Nectar. Moisture at mudpuddles.

GARDENING SUGGESTIONS: Very likely in your garden. Plant pipevines. Native species: Dutchman's pipevine, in most of the East; Watson's pipevine from West Texas to Arizona; California pipevine in California. The tropical species, Elegant pipevine in Florida and southern Texas.

ABUNDANCE: Uncommon to locally common. Flight is throughout warmer months.

ETC.: The growth of butterfly gardening will make these species more common.

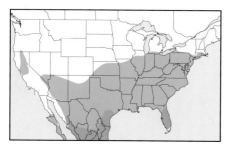

○ **Range of Polydamas Swallowtail.**
● **Range of Pipevine Swallowtail.**
● **Range where both are found.**

Opposite: Polydamas Swallowtail. ***Above:*** Pipevine Swallowtail obtaining salts at damp sand.
Above inset: Pipevine Swallowtail caterpillar.

Kite-Swallowtails No. of species: 1

LENGTH OF FOREWING: ───────

HOW TO KNOW THEM: Although their last name is "swallowtail," Zebra Swallowtails are actually part of the kite-swallowtail group, named for their triangular, kite-like wings. With their black and white stripes and long tails, Zebra Swallowtails are easy to identify. A bright red stripe stands out on the underside of the wings. It is likely that, in the future, the NABA Names Committee will change the name of this and other species to match the groups they are in. For example, this species will become Zebra Kite-Swallowtail and Gray Hairstreak will become Gray Scrub-Hairstreak (see page 104).

WHERE THEY LIVE: Open brushy areas and woodland edges with pawpaws.

WHAT THE CATERPILLARS EAT: Pawpaws.

WHAT THE ADULTS EAT: Nectar. Moisture at mudpuddles.

GARDENING SUGGESTIONS: Likely in gardens. Plant pawpaws for the caterpillars and orange milkweed for the adults.

ABUNDANCE: Usually uncommon, but can be common in the right habitat. Flight is throughout the warmer months.

ETC.: Flight is usually low to the ground, fast, and erratic. Spring individuals are usually smaller, with shorter tails, than are summer individuals. Occasionally there is a temporary range expansion, but the real range is limited by the occurrence of pawpaws. This is the official butterfly of a number of states.

● **Range of Zebra Swallowtail, 2 flights.**
● **Range of Zebra Swallowtail, 3 flights.**

Opposite: A Zebra Swallowtail nectaring at orange milkweed. ***Above:*** A Zebra Swallowtail nectaring at Spanish needles.

"Black" Swallowtails No. of species: 6

LENGTH OF FOREWING: ━━━━━━━━━━━━

HOW TO KNOW THEM: These are large, black butterflies with distinctive tails. The males of some species also have considerable amounts of yellow on their wings. Species include Anise, Black, Indra, Old World, Ozark, and Short-tailed swallowtails.

WHERE THEY LIVE: Most species live in open areas, such as fields and roadsides. Habitats of some include disturbed areas, such as suburban developments; also found in arid and semi-arid areas.

WHAT THE CATERPILLARS EAT: Mainly plants in the parsley family.

WHAT THE ADULTS EAT: Nectar.

GARDENING SUGGESTIONS: Very likely in gardens. Plant fennel and parsley.

ABUNDANCE: Mainly uncommon to common. In the East, flight of Black Swallowtails is throughout the warmer months. In the West, Anise Swallowtail flies mainly May–July, longer along the coast. Other species are less common.

ETC.: The green-and-black banded caterpillars are very showy. Most of the species are strong hilltoppers and that is where some of the western species are most likely to be found.

● **Range of "black" swallowtails.**

Opposite: A Black Swallowtail nectaring at mistflower. **Above:** Anise Swallowtail.

"Giant" Swallowtails   No. of species: 2

LENGTH OF FOREWING: ━━━━━━━━━━━━━━━━━━━━━━━━━

HOW TO KNOW THEM: As their name implies, Giant Swallowtails are large. In flight, their cream-colored underwings contrast with their dark brown (almost black) topsides. Similar in appearance but not closely related, Palamedes Swallowtails are also very large, but they are brown below and the yellow bands above are differently patterned.

WHERE THEY LIVE: Giant Swallowtail in open woodlands and gardens; Schaus' Swallowtail in tropical hardwood hammocks on the Florida Keys.

WHAT THE CATERPILLARS EAT: Citrus-family plants.

WHAT THE ADULTS EAT: Nectar.

GARDENING SUGGESTIONS: Very possible in your garden, especially in the South. Try lemon, wild lime, and Hercules' Club southward, prickly ash and hoptree northward.

ABUNDANCE: Schaus' Swallowtail is rare and endangered. Giant Swallowtail is common in the South, becoming uncommon to rare northward. Giant Swallowtail's flight is throughout the warmer months. Schaus' Swallowtail's flight is mainly May–June.

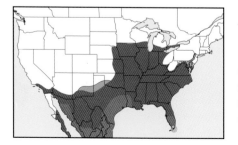

ETC.: Giant Swallowtails are a minor nuisance to citrus growers, who refer to the caterpillars as orange dogs.

● **Range of Giant Swallowtail, 1 flight.**
● **Range of Giant Swallowtail, 2 flights.**
● **Range of Giant Swallowtails, 3 flights.**
● **Range where both Giant and Schaus' Swallowtails are found.**

Opposite: A Giant Swallowtail showing its underside as it nectars at a thistle. *Above:* A Giant Swallowtail showing its topside. *Above inset:* Giant Swallowtail caterpillar.

Tiger Swallowtails No. of species: 5

LENGTH OF FOREWING: ━━━━━━━━━━━━━━━━

HOW TO KNOW THEM: These are very large, yellow-and-black striped butterflies with distinctive tails. Their name reminds you of their appearance. All five species are very similar looking.

WHERE THEY LIVE: Open woodlands, wooded suburban areas, wooded watercourses.

WHAT THE CATERPILLARS EAT: A variety of trees, including wild black cherry, tulip-tree, bays, aspens, and ashes.

WHAT THE ADULTS EAT: Nectar. Moisture at mudpuddles.

GARDENING SUGGESTIONS: Very likely in your garden. For the caterpillars: Wild black cherry in the East, ash in the West, sweet bay in the South. For adults: try aromatic Oriental lily hybrids.

ABUNDANCE: Common. Flight is throughout the warmer months.

ETC.: Some female Eastern Tiger Swallowtails, especially common in the South, are almost completely black. They retain a ghost of the tiger pattern.

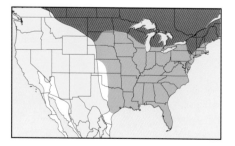

○ Range of Two-tailed, Pale, and Western Tiger Swallowtails.

● Range of Canadian Tiger Swallowtail.

● Range of Eastern Tiger Swallowtail.

Opposite: A platoon of Two-tailed Swallowtails mudpuddling. ***Above:*** An Eastern Tiger Swallowtail nectaring at swamp milkweed.

Spicebush & Palamedes Swallowtails No. of species: 2

LENGTH OF FOREWING: ━━━━━━━━━━━━━━

HOW TO KNOW THEM: Our two species of laurel-feeding swallowtails are closely related but seem quite different. Spicebush Swallowtails resemble Black Swallowtails, but have green tones above. Palamedes Swallowtails are dark brown and yellow, like Giant Swallowtails, but below they are dark brown with a yellow stripe, not cream-colored, as are Giant Swallowtails.

WHERE THEY LIVE: Spicebush in open woodlands and woodland edges, Palamedes mainly in swamp margins and adjacent areas.

WHAT THE CATERPILLARS EAT: Laurel family plants, especially sassafras and spicebush for Spicebush and red bay for Palamedes.

WHAT THE ADULTS EAT: Nectar. Moisture at mudpuddles.

GARDENING SUGGESTIONS: Very possible in your garden. Plant sassafras northward and red bay southward.

ABUNDANCE: Mainly common. Flight is throughout the warmer months.

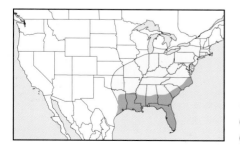

Range of Spicebush Swallowtail.
Range of Palamedes Swallowtail.
Range where both occur.

Opposite: A Spicebush Swallowtail nectaring at swamp milkweed. ***Above:*** A Palamedes Swallowtail nectaring at thistle. ***Above inset:*** Spicebush Swallowtail caterpillar.

Parnassians   No. of species: 2

LENGTH OF FOREWING: ━━━━━━━━━

HOW TO KNOW THEM: Their large size, shortened wings, large bodies, and the usual presence of red spots on their wings, separate this untailed, specialized group of swallowtails from the whites.

WHERE THEY LIVE: Mainly moist mountain meadows and rocky summits.

WHAT THE CATERPILLARS EAT: Phoebus Parnassians eat stonecrops. Clodius Parnassians eat bleeding-hearts.

WHAT THE ADULTS EAT: Nectar.

GARDENING SUGGESTIONS: Not normally in gardens, but if your land is in the right mountain habitat, planting stonecrops or bleeding hearts might work.

ABUNDANCE: Mainly common. Flight is mainly June–August.

ETC.: Many parnassian species are found in isolated, relatively inaccessible, mountain-top habitats throughout the Northern Hemisphere.

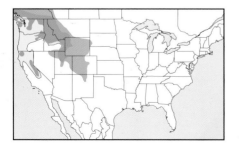

● **Range of Clodius Parnassian.**
● **Range of Phoebus Parnassian.**
● **Range where both are found.**

Opposite: A Phoebus Parnassian nectaring at stonecrop. ***Above:*** A Clodius Parnassian nectaring at bindweed.

"Pine" Whites   No. of species: 2

LENGTH OF FOREWING: ▬▬▬▬▬

HOW TO KNOW THEM: Floating high among the pines, these whites are perhaps the most graceful aeronauts of any of the North American butterflies. When seen clearly, the black pattern on the forewing is unlike that of any other butterflies. The females of Chiricahua White, found only in extreme southeastern Arizona, have a pattern similar to males, but the areas of white are replaced by bold orange.

WHERE THEY LIVE: Pine forests.

WHAT THE CATERPILLARS EAT: Ponderosa pines, other pine family trees.

WHAT THE ADULTS EAT: Nectar and moisture at damp sand.

GARDENING SUGGESTIONS: Unlikely to be in your garden, unless you live among the pines.

ABUNDANCE: Common to abundant in their preferred habitats, Pine Whites fly mainly July–September, while Chiricahua Whites fly through October.

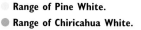
● **Range of Pine White.**
● **Range of Chiricahua White.**

Opposite: A Pine White nectaring at wood sorrel. *Top left:* Chiricahua White, male. *Top right:* Pine White. *Bottom:* Chiricahua White, female.

"Checkered" Whites   No. of species: 4

LENGTH OF FOREWING: ━━━━━━━━━

HOW TO KNOW THEM: These are medium-sized white butterflies with brown/black blotches on the forewings above, especially in the middle of the forewing cell. Below, the veins are outlined in greenish-yellow, shading to gray.

WHERE THEY LIVE: Widespread in open areas, especially in and near agricultural areas and very disturbed habitats. Becker's Whites live in arid areas, especially sagebrush lands. Spring Whites are most easily found on western hilltops.

WHAT THE CATERPILLARS EAT: A wide variety of plants in the mustard family.

WHAT THE ADULTS EAT: Nectar.

GARDENING SUGGESTIONS: Possible in your garden. Try peppergrass.

ABUNDANCE: Checkered Whites are most common in lowlands, common to abundant in much of the south, rare to uncommon northward. They fly through the warmer months. Western Whites are found mainly in the western mountains and are usually uncommon. Mostly their flight is from April–September, but only July–August at high elevations.

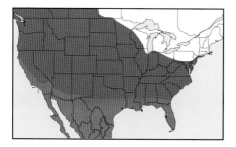

ETC.: Previously, agricultural land was common in the Northeast, and Checkered Whites were common. Now they are scarce there but have become more common throughout the West.

● **Range of "checkered" whites, 2 flights.**
● **Range of "checkered" whites, 3 flights.**

Opposite: A Checkered White nectaring at Spanish needles. ***Above:*** A Western White nectaring at rabbitbrush.

"Cabbage and Mustard" Whites   No. of species: 3

LENGTH OF FOREWING: ━━━━━━━━━━

HOW TO KNOW THEM: These medium-sized white butterflies lack extensive black areas along the wing margins that "checkered" whites have. Female Cabbage Whites have two black spots on their forewings while males have one spot.

WHERE THEY LIVE: Gardens, roadsides, fields, agricultural areas and other disturbed areas for Cabbage Whites. Moist deciduous or coniferous forest for Mustard and West Virginia Whites.

WHAT THE CATERPILLARS EAT: A wide variety of mustard family plants.

WHAT THE ADULTS EAT: Nectar.

GARDENING SUGGESTIONS: Cabbage Whites are very likely to be in your garden. Plant cabbage, broccoli, and nasturtium.

ABUNDANCE: Common to abundant. Flight is throughout the warmer months.

ETC.: Cabbage White is a European species that became established in Canada in the nineteenth century and is now the most ubiquitous butterfly in the United States. Unlike most butterflies, they thrive in suburban and disturbed areas and fly even in midtown Manhattan. Their graceful flight brings the beauty of butterflies to many areas that would otherwise be lifeless.

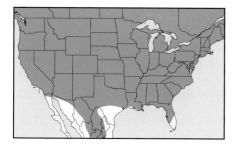

● **Range of "cabbage and mustard" whites.**

Opposite left: Mustard White. ***Opposite right:*** A female Cabbage White nectaring at Canada thistle. ***Above:*** A male Cabbage White nectaring at orange sparkler zinnia.

Marbles   No. of species: 4

LENGTH OF FOREWING: ━━━━━━━

HOW TO KNOW THEM: Marbles are smallish white butterflies that have beautiful green, or yellow-green, marbling below. If you get a close look at them, you can see that their eyes are green. Unfortunately for us, they fly more often than they sit. Species include Gray, Large, Olympia, and Pearly marbles.

WHERE THEY LIVE: A wide variety of open habitats, including mountain meadows, roadsides, chaparral, sagebrush, and desert washes. In the East, more restricted to limestone or sand barrens.

WHAT THE CATERPILLARS EAT: Rock cresses and other crucifers.

WHAT THE ADULTS EAT: Nectar.

GARDENING SUGGESTIONS: They're not very likely to be in your garden, but you could plant rock cresses and hope.

ABUNDANCE: Mainly uncommon to common, but in the Pacific Northwest, Large Marble can be abundant. Marbles have one flight per year, in the spring or early summer.

ETC.: Olympia Marble is the only marble in the Midwest and East.

● **Range of marbles.**

Opposite: Large Marble. **Above:** An Olympia Marble on birdfoot violet (posed photo).

Orangetips   No. of species: 3

LENGTH OF FOREWING: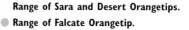

HOW TO KNOW THEM: Those bright orange wingtips don't lie! These early spring bursts of color are a wake-up call for overwintering butterfliers. Female Falcate Orangetips lack the orange wingtips, but can be recognized by the unusual shape of their forewing.

WHERE THEY LIVE: Mainly open woodlands for Falcate Orangetip, desert hills for Desert Orangetip, and a great variety of habitats for Sara Orangetip.

WHAT THE CATERPILLARS EAT: Many crucifers.

WHAT THE ADULTS EAT: Nectar.

GARDENING SUGGESTIONS: Not very likely to be in your garden, but rock cresses and other cresses, such as *Cardamines*, couldn't hurt.

ABUNDANCE: Mainly common. Flying in the early spring, which can be February in southern California and July in the Colorado mountains.

ETC.: Desert Orangetips are strong hilltoppers, Sara Orangetips are not. Falcate Orangetips fly low to the ground, Desert and Sara Orangetips fly higher.

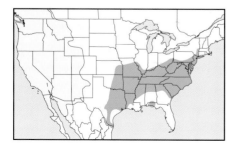

Range of Sara and Desert Orangetips.
Range of Falcate Orangetip.

Opposite: Falcate Orangetips mating on sicklepod, a caterpillar foodplant. The female is on the left.

Above: A Sara Orangetip nectaring at sticky yerba santa.

Sulphurs   No. of species: 12

LENGTH OF FOREWING: ───────

HOW TO KNOW THEM: Sulphurs are medium-sized butterflies. Although they always keep their wings closed while landed, it is easy to see their bright yellow or orange topsides in flight. Clouded Sulphurs are bright yellow above, lacking any orange, while Orange Sulphurs have at least some orange above.

WHERE THEY LIVE: The most common and widespread species are found in open fields, agricultural areas, roadsides, etc. The less common species are found in more specialized northern habitats.

WHAT THE CATERPILLARS EAT: The most common and widespread species eat legumes; other species eat mainly blueberries and related plants.

WHAT THE ADULTS EAT: Nectar.

GARDENING SUGGESTIONS: Very likely to be in your garden. Try alfalfa and clovers.

ABUNDANCE: Orange and Clouded Sulphurs are mainly common to abundant, and are the only species found throughout almost the entire East and much of the West. They fly throughout warm weather. Most of the other species—Christina's, Giant, Labrador, Mead's, Pelidne, Pink-edged, Scudder's, Sierra, Queen Alexandra's, and Western sulphurs—are found in the high mountains or the far North.

ETC.: Even experts disagree about the taxonomy of many of these butterflies.

● **Range of sulphurs.**

Opposite: An Orange Sulphur nectaring at sunflower. *Top:* A Mead's Sulphur nectaring at an aster. *Bottom:* A Pink-edged Sulphur nectaring at leafy-headed aster.

Dogfaces   No. of species: 2

LENGTH OF FOREWING: ━━━━━━━━━━━━

HOW TO KNOW THEM: Somewhat larger than related sulphurs, dogfaces have more pointed forewings and have a bold dogface pattern on the topside of their forewings. Although they do not open their wings when landed (unless forced to — by a spider for example), the dogface pattern can usually be seen through the wing, even when the butterfly is landed. The two species are very similar, but male California Dogfaces have a violet sheen when fresh (that is, when they've recently emerged from the chrysalis).

WHERE THEY LIVE: Mainly dry open areas, including agricultural lands. California Dogface in mountain canyons and meadows.

WHAT THE CATERPILLARS EAT: False indigo and other legumes.

WHAT THE ADULTS EAT: Nectar.

GARDENING SUGGESTIONS: False indigo and kidneywood.

ABUNDANCE: Mainly uncommon, but Southern Dogface can be abundant in southern Texas. Southern Dogface is mainly a late-season immigrant to the northern parts of its range.

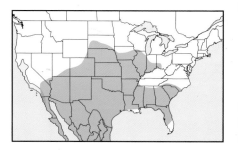

● **Range of California Dogface.**
● **Range of Southern Dogface.**
● **Range where both are found.**

Opposite: Southern Dogface. **Top:** A Southern Dogface caught by a green lynx spider (with babies).
Bottom: Southern Dogface caterpillar.

Giant-Sulphurs No. of species: 4

LENGTH OF FOREWING: ━━━━━━━━━━━━━

HOW TO KNOW THEM: Giant-sulphurs are very large and bright yellow or orange on their topsides (one can see a bit of the forewing topside on the individual shown on the next page). Most individuals have two large pale spots in the middle of the underside of the hindwing. Their flight is swift. Although also large and yellow, tiger swallowtails have black stripes and tails. Monarchs are colored orange-brown.

WHERE THEY LIVE: Open areas, especially woodland edges, roadsides, and gardens.

WHAT THE CATERPILLARS EAT: Mainly sennas and various legumes.

WHAT THE ADULTS EAT: Nectar

GARDENING SUGGESTIONS: Very likely to be in your garden in the southern part of the range shown. Try various sennas; species will depend upon your location.

ABUNDANCE: Common to abundant in the southern part of the range shown. Northward, one finds late-season immigrants, especially of Cloudless Sulphur, which is by far the most common and wide-ranging species.

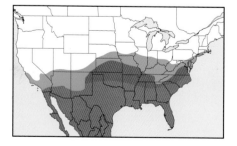

● **Range of giant-sulphurs, 1 flight.**
● **Range of giant-sulphurs, 2 flights.**
● **Range of giant-sulphurs, 3 flights.**

Opposite: A Cloudless Sulphur nectaring at morning-glory. *Above:* An Orange-barred Sulphur nectaring at shrimp plant. *Above inset:* Cloudless Sulphur pupa.

Yellows   No. of species: 7

LENGTH OF FOREWING: ▬▬▬▬▬▬

HOW TO KNOW THEM: Yellows are small, with bright yellow topsides. Flight is low to the ground and not as strong as the somewhat similar looking sulphurs. If you get a good look at them, you can often see that yellows' antennas are black and white, whereas sulphurs' antennas are mainly pink. Species include Barred, Boisduval's, Dina, Ghost, Little, Mexican, and Mimosa yellows.

WHERE THEY LIVE: A wide variety of open areas.

WHAT THE CATERPILLARS EAT: Mainly sennas and legumes.

WHAT THE ADULTS EAT: Nectar.

GARDENING SUGGESTIONS: Possible in your garden. Try cassias, such as Chapman's senna and Christmas senna.

ABUNDANCE: Common to abundant in the southern part of range shown. Most species are tropical, barely entering the United States. Only Little Yellow, in the East, and Mexican Yellow, in the West, are found in much of the country, and even they are late-season immigrants, decreasing as one moves northward.

ETC.: Yellows and oranges (shown on the next two-page spread) are very closely related taxonomically and are distinguished, only operationally, by their color.

● **Range of yellows.**

Opposite: A Mexican Yellow nectaring at thistle. ***Above:*** A Dina Yellow nectaring at cheese-shrub.

Oranges & Dainty Sulphur   No. of species: 2 + 1

LENGTH OF FOREWING, ORANGES: ━━━━━━━
LENGTH OF FOREWING, DAINTY SULPHUR: ━━━━━

HOW TO KNOW THEM: Oranges are small with bright orange topsides. Dainty Sulphur is very small with a pale yellow upperside and a greenish underside. Underside of forewing has two bold black spots.

WHERE THEY LIVE: A wide variety of open areas, including arid regions, prairies, and open woodlands.

WHAT THE CATERPILLARS EAT: Sennas and aster family plants, respectively.

WHAT THE ADULTS EAT: Nectar.

GARDENING SUGGESTIONS: Possible in your garden. Plant sennas for oranges, Bidens and other aster family plants for Dainty Sulphur.

ABUNDANCE: Sleepy Orange and Dainty Sulphur are common southward; their abundance decreases as one moves northward, where they are late-season immigrants. Tailed Orange barely enters the U.S. in extreme southern Texas and southeastern Arizona.

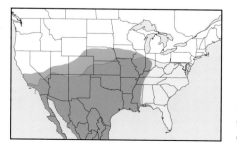

Range of oranges.
Range of Dainty Sulphur.
Range where both are found.

Opposite: A Sleepy Orange nectaring at a composite. ***Above:*** Tailed Orange. ***Above inset:*** A Dainty Sulphur nectaring at phacelia.

Harvester   No. of species: I

LENGTH OF FOREWING: ━━━━━

HOW TO KNOW THEM: Harvester adults are small and appear to be finespun, belying their fierce caterpillar past. With their bright orange and black topside they can only reasonably be confused with American Coppers. But Harvesters have orange-brown underwings, laced with delicate white markings, while American Coppers have pale gray hindwings below.

WHERE THEY LIVE: Mainly in moist woodlands with alders.

WHAT THE CATERPILLARS EAT: Wooly aphids.

WHAT THE ADULTS EAT: Moisture at damp sand.

GARDENING SUGGESTIONS: Not likely to be in your garden.

ABUNDANCE: Rare to uncommon, with two or three flights per year, from April or May to September or October.

ETC.: Harvester is the only North American butterfly that has carniverous caterpillars — the caterpillars feed on aphids rather than on plants. In other parts of the world there are other carniverous caterpillars, including close relatives of Harvester and certain blues that eat the ants that take care of them.

● **Range of Harvester.**

Opposite: Two Harvester caterpillars (at center, long and gray) among aphids. ***Above:*** A Harvester obtains salts from damp sand.

Coppers   No. of species: 16

LENGTH OF FOREWING: ━━━━━

HOW TO KNOW THEM: Coppers are small but sensational gems of the butterfly world. Examples are shown on this and the next five pages. First, recognize them as gossamer-wings by their very small size and distinctive wing shape (other very small butterflies, such as skippers, have different wing shapes). Then, with more experience, recognize that they aren't blues or hairstreaks. Tailed Copper is the only copper with tails. Other species include American, Blue, Bog, Bronze, Dorcas, Edith's, Gorgon, Gray, Great, Hermes, Lilac-bordered, Lustrous, Mariposa, Purplish, and Ruddy coppers.

WHERE THEY LIVE: A wide variety of open habitats.

WHAT THE CATERPILLARS EAT: The majority of species eat docks and knotweeds while the remainder use a variety of other plants. Tailed Copper eats gooseberries.

WHAT THE ADULTS EAT: Nectar.

GARDENING SUGGESTIONS: Not likely to be in your garden, unless you live adjacent to a wild population.

ABUNDANCE: American Copper is the only widespread, common copper in the East. Most species are uncommon, but some can be common, even abundant, in their specific habitats.

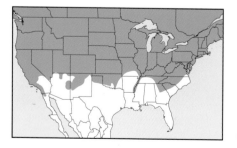

● **Range of coppers.**

Opposite: An American Copper nectaring at beach plum. **Above:** A Tailed Copper at sulphur buckwheat.

Coppers (continued)

LENGTH OF FOREWING: ━━━━━━━━

HOW TO KNOW THEM: Many coppers, especially females, have a pattern of black spots on the uppersides that is very similar to that of Purplish Copper. Blue Coppers could be mistaken for blues, but are much larger.

WHERE THEY LIVE: A wide variety of open habitats.

WHAT THE CATERPILLARS EAT: The majority of species eat docks and knotweeds while the remainder use a variety of other plants. Purplish Coppers eat docks and knotweeds. Blue Coppers eat buckwheats.

WHAT THE ADULTS EAT: Nectar.

GARDENING SUGGESTIONS: Not really garden butterflies, but you should plant buckwheats anyway, since they are important butterfly garden plants.

ABUNDANCE: Purplish Copper is the most widespread, common copper in the West, but Blue Copper is also widespread and can be common. Purplish Coppers have two to three flights per year, depending upon location, flying through much of the warmer months. Blue Coppers have a single summer flight.

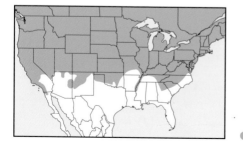

● **Range of coppers.**

Opposite: Purplish Copper. ***Above:*** Blue Copper.

Coppers (continued)

LENGTH OF FOREWING: ▬▬▬▬▬

HOW TO KNOW THEM: The iridescent orange or purple of most species of coppers is distinctive. In general, as with the Ruddy Copper shown on these pages, female coppers are duller than the males. If you see the underside, the bold black spots on the forewings are a useful clue that you are viewing a copper, although some blues also have these spots.

WHERE THEY LIVE: A wide variety of open habitats.

WHAT THE CATERPILLARS EAT: The majority of species, including the two shown here, eat docks and knotweeds while the remainder use a variety of other plants.

WHAT THE ADULTS EAT: Nectar.

GARDENING SUGGESTIONS: Not likely to be in your garden unless you live adjacent to a wild population.

ABUNDANCE: Both Ruddy and Lilac-bordered Coppers can be common in mountain meadows, but Ruddy Coppers are found in moist meadows in arid country, while the homeland of Lilac-bordered Coppers is the Pacific Northwest.

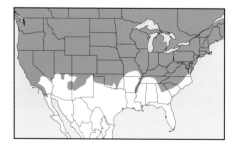

● **Range of coppers.**

Opposite: Ruddy Copper female. **Top:** A Lilac-bordered Copper nectaring at pussypaws.
Bottom: Ruddy Copper male.

Golden & Colorado Hairstreaks No. of species: 1 + 1

LENGTH OF FOREWING: ━━━━━━━━

HOW TO KNOW THEM: Golden and Colorado Hairstreaks are large — for hairstreaks. Golden Hairstreaks have unusual ice-blue markings near the hindwing margin. Colorado Hairstreaks are a stunning purple color above (unfortunately rendered as blue by Kodachrome).

WHERE THEY LIVE: Canyons with oaks. Golden Hairstreak also is found in chaparral.

WHAT THE CATERPILLARS EAT: Canyon oak and chinquapin for Golden Hairstreak, Gambel's oak for Colorado Hairstreak.

WHAT THE ADULTS EAT: These species nectar less frequently than do other hairstreaks.

GARDENING SUGGESTIONS: Not likely to be in your garden.

ABUNDANCE: Mainly uncommon.

ETC.: These species are more closely related to Old World hairstreaks than they are to any of the other 1000 species found in the New World. Unlike most New World hairstreaks, Golden and Colorado Hairstreaks will perch with their wings held open.

● Range of Colorado Hairstreak.
● Range of Golden Hairstreak.
● Range where both are found.

Opposite: Golden Hairstreak. ***Above:*** Colorado Hairstreak.

Atala & Great Purple Hairstreaks   No. of species: 1 + 1

LENGTH OF FOREWING: ━━━━━━━━━

HOW TO KNOW THEM: Both Great Purple Hairstreak and Atala are large and brilliant. Both have orange abdomens, red spots near the base of the undersides of their wings and iridescent blue on their topsides, particularly brilliant on Great Purple Hairstreaks.

WHERE THEY LIVE: Anyplace that has their foodplants.

WHAT THE CATERPILLARS EAT: Atalas eat coontie (native) and introduced cycads. Great Purple Hairstreaks eat mistletoes.

WHAT THE ADULTS EAT: Nectar.

GARDENING SUGGESTIONS: Atala is very likely to be in your garden — if you live in southern Florida. Plant coontie, or ornamental cycads. Great Purple Hairstreak is possible but propagating mistletoe is a bit of a challenge.

ABUNDANCE: Atala is usually common but is erratic — it can be rare or abundant. Great Purple Hairstreaks are mainly uncommon.

ETC.: Atala was thought possibly to be extinct in the 1970s, but with the surging use of ornamental cycads as landscape plants, it is now flourishing.

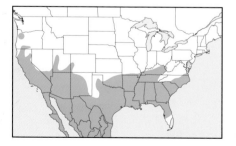

Range of Atala.
Range of Great Purple Hairstreak.

Opposite: Atala. ***Opposite inset:*** An Atala caterpillar on its foodplant, coontie. ***Above:*** A Great Purple Hairstreak nectaring at desert lavender.

Satyrium Hairstreaks   No. of species: 17

LENGTH OF FOREWING: ━━━━━

HOW TO KNOW THEM: Most are brownish-gray in coloration, with a blue spot on the hindwing near the tail and with a pattern resembling one of the two species shown. Species include Acadian, Banded, Behr's, California, Coral, Edwards', Gold-hunter's, Hedgerow, Hickory, Ilavia, King's, Mountain Mahogany, Oak, Poling's, Sooty, Striped, and Sylvan hairstreaks.

WHERE THEY LIVE: Most species inhabit woodland openings and brushy edges, but they also can be found in chaparral and sagebrush.

WHAT THE CATERPILLARS EAT: About one-half the species eat oaks. Others eat willows, black cherries, and other plants.

WHAT THE ADULTS EAT: Nectar.

GARDENING SUGGESTIONS: If you are near woodlands, even in suburbia, small oaks or wild black cherries may be attractive. Coral Hairstreaks are particularly fond of orange milkweed as an adult nectar source.

ABUNDANCE: Many of the species are common in the right habitat. Each species has only one flight per year, mainly in early to midsummer.

ETC.: The caterpillars of many of these butterflies live in association with ants (see the Introduction, page 32). Some of them leave the ant nest only after dusk, climbing small oaks with a phalanx of ants.

● **Range of *Satyrium* hairstreaks.**

Opposite: Hedgerow Hairstreak. ***Above:*** A Coral Hairstreak at rabbitbrush. ***Above inset:*** An Edwards' Hairstreak caterpillar climbs a scrub oak to feed, just after dusk, attended by ants.

Elfins   No. of species: 9

LENGTH OF FOREWING: ▬▬▬

HOW TO KNOW THEM: First, recognize them as hairstreaks by their wing shape and general color pattern. Most species have checkered fringes, a feature that few other hairstreaks share. In addition, they fly in the early spring, when few other species will be encountered. Species include Bog, Brown, Eastern Pine, Frosted, Henry's, Hoary, Desert, Moss', and Western Pine elfins.

WHERE THEY LIVE: Mainly in barrens and other stressed habitats, such as rocky outcrops and bogs, but Western Pine Elfins are widely distributed in pine forests.

WHAT THE CATERPILLARS EAT: Most species eat only particular groups of plants— different for each species. For example, the pine elfins eat pines while Hoary Elfins eat bearberry. But Brown Elfins will eat a wide variety of plants.

WHAT THE ADULTS EAT: Nectar.

GARDENING SUGGESTIONS: Not likely to be in your garden.

ABUNDANCE: Most species are uncommon; Brown Elfins and the pine elfins are the most widespread. Elfins have only one flight each year, usually in the very early spring, but in some areas pine elfins can still be flying as late as early July.

Range of elfins.

Opposite: Brown Elfin. ***Above:*** A Western Pine Elfin guards its territory.

Cedar Hairstreaks   No. of species: 2

LENGTH OF FOREWING: ━━━━━

HOW TO KNOW THEM: There are only two species of cedar/juniper-feeding hairstreaks. In the East, Hessel's Hairstreak and Juniper Hairstreak are both green and very similar. In the far West, populations of Juniper Hairstreaks are brown and some have purple sheens. But only cedar hairstreaks and two closely related species have three small black spots in a straight line on the outer hindwing.

WHERE THEY LIVE: Juniper Hairstreaks live almost anyplace their cedar and juniper foodplants are found. Hessel's Hairstreak is restricted to Atlantic white cedar swamps.

WHAT THE CATERPILLARS EAT: Atlantic white cedar for Hessel's Hairstreak. Juniper Hairstreak uses junipers in most of its range; in the far West, incense cedar, Sargent's cypress, and Tecate cypress are used by some populations.

WHAT THE ADULTS EAT: Nectar.

GARDENING SUGGESTIONS: Juniper Hairstreak is possible in your garden. Plant Eastern red cedar in the East, try various other native junipers in the West.

ABUNDANCE: Juniper Hairstreak is often common in the right habitat. In much of its range there is a spring flight and a mid-summer flight. Hessel's Hairstreak is rare.

◯ **Range of Hessel's Hairstreak.**

● **Range of Juniper Hairstreak.**

● **Range where both are found.**

Opposite: 'Nelson's' Juniper Hairstreak, a western subspecies of Juniper Hairstreak. ***Above:*** A Hessel's Hairstreak nectaring at sand myrtle.

Scrub-Hairstreaks   No. of species: 9

LENGTH OF FOREWING: ▬▬▬▬▬

HOW TO KNOW THEM: Species include Gray Hairstreak, as well as Avalon, Bartram's, Lantana, Lacey's, Mallow, Martial, Red-crescent, and Yojoa scrub-hairstreak. Gray Hairstreak is usually a true gray color, not brown. On the hindwing there is a line of white dashes, with black dashes inside of them. Many individuals also have red dashes just inside the black dashes.

WHERE THEY LIVE: A wide variety of open habitats, especially in disturbed areas.

WHAT THE CATERPILLARS EAT: Gray Hairstreaks will eat many different plants in different plant families. Some of the other scrub-hairstreaks are more restricted. For example, Mallow Scrub-Hairstreak uses mallow family plants while Bartram's Scrub-Hairstreak eats only narrow-leaved croton.

WHAT THE ADULTS EAT: Nectar.

GARDENING SUGGESTIONS: Gray Hairstreak is a garden possibility. Try alfalfa, white clover, globemallows, and garden beans and peas.

ABUNDANCE: Gray Hairstreak is mainly common in the South, becoming uncommon farther north. Flight is throughout the warmer months. Other scrub-hairstreaks are rare to uncommon and are restricted to southern Florida and/or Texas.

ETC.: Primarily tropical, scrub-hairstreaks are one of few groups of U.S. hairstreaks that sometimes perch with wings open.

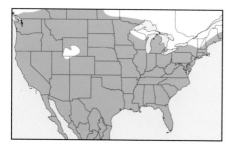

● **Range of scrub-hairstreaks.**

Opposite: Gray Hairstreak. **Above:** A Mallow Scrub-Hairstreak nectaring at coral vine. **Above inset:** A Martial Scrub-Hairstreak caterpillar on its foodplant, bay cedar.

Pygmy-Blues & Black-eyed Blues   No. of species: 2 + 7

LENGTH OF FOREWING: ▬▬▬▬

HOW TO KNOW THEM: These tiny butterflies reward close observation. The undersides of the hindwings, near the margins, have black eyespots that contain beautiful irides-cent gemming. The number of spots ranges from one to four. Pygmy-blues include Eastern and Western pygmy-blues (the smallest North American butterfly). Black-eyed blues include Cassius, Ceraunus, Cyna, Marine, Miami, Nickerbean, and Reakirt's blues.

WHERE THEY LIVE: Pygmy-blues are found in salt marsh tidal flats in the East, and in arid country with saltbush in the West. Black-eyed blues inhabit open areas, from low desert to suburbia to open woodland.

WHAT THE CATERPILLARS EAT: Pygmy-blues eat glasswort and saltbush. Black-eyed blues eat many plants (mainly their flowers), especially legumes.

WHAT THE ADULTS EAT: Nectar.

GARDENING SUGGESTIONS: Possible in your garden. Try butterfly pea or various species of kidneywood.

ABUNDANCE: Many of the species are common to abundant, but because they are so small they can easily be overlooked.

ETC.: Marine Blue and Reakirt's Blue occasionally have population explosions that take them far northward.

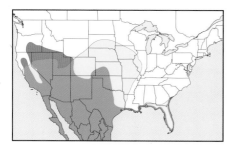

● **Range of black-eyed blues.**
● **Range of pygmy-blues.**
● **Range where both are found.**

Opposite: Marine Blue male. *Above:* A Ceraunus Blue nectaring at stinging cevallia.
Above inset: Western Pygmy-Blue.

Tailed-Blues No. of species: 2

LENGTH OF FOREWING: ━━━━━

HOW TO KNOW THEM: Males, bright blue above with tailed hindwings, are obvious because tailed-blues are the only North American blues with tails. Females, which are dull blue-gray above, could be confused with hairstreaks, but are smaller. Also, the flight of hairstreaks is usually very rapid and directional, while that of blues is weaker with more hovering.

WHERE THEY LIVE: A wide variety of open areas. Eastern Tailed-Blues are most often found in lowland, disturbed habitats. Westerns favor more pristine situations.

WHAT THE CATERPILLARS EAT: Legumes.

WHAT THE ADULTS EAT: Nectar.

GARDENING SUGGESTIONS: Possible in your garden. Try garden peas.

ABUNDANCE: Eastern Tailed-Blues, flying throughout the warmer months, are common to abundant in much of the East, rare in the West; Western Tailed-Blues, flying mainly in the spring, are usually uncommon.

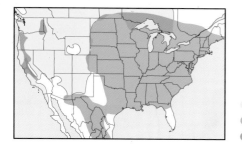

● **Range of Western Tailed-Blue.**
● **Range of Eastern Tailed-Blue.**
● **Range where both are found.**

Opposite: Western Tailed-Blue. ***Above:*** Eastern Tailed-Blue.

Azures   No. of species: 3

LENGTH OF FOREWING: ━━━━

HOW TO KNOW THEM: All three species are very similar. Unlike most other blues, azures have no orange markings and lack strong black spots. Some spring-flying populations of Spring Azures have dark brown hindwing blotches in the center of the hindwing underside and/or a hindwing brown border.

WHERE THEY LIVE: Woodlands, mainly open, including woodland edges and suburbia.

WHAT THE CATERPILLARS EAT: A wide variety of shrubs and trees.

WHAT THE ADULTS EAT: Nectar. Moisture at mudpuddles.

GARDENING SUGGESTIONS: Likely in your garden.

ABUNDANCE: The widespread Spring Azure is often common, sometimes abundant, flying throughout the warmer months. Appalachian and Dusky Azures are range-restricted and rare to uncommon, flying only in mid-spring.

ETC.: One of the first butterflies to emerge in the spring, the Spring Azure complex includes a bewildering array of populations. Because many of these populations are adapted to use particular caterpillar foodplants, they emerge at slightly different times than do nearby populations. The relationships between these populations are still being sorted out.

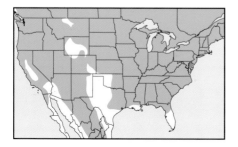

● **Range of azures.**

Opposite: Spring Azure. ***Above:*** Spring Azure.

"Silvery" & *Plebejus* Blues   No. of species: 2 + 7

LENGTH OF FOREWING, "SILVERY" BLUES: ━━━━━━━━
LENGTH OF FOREWING, *PLEBEJUS* BLUES: ━━━━━━

HOW TO KNOW THEM: Arrowhead Blue, closely related to Silvery Blue, is distinctive, having hindwing white markings in the shape of arrowheads. Silvery Blue is without these white markings, has a very strong row of black spots on both forewing and hindwing, but lacks black spots near the wing margins. In contrast, Boisduval's Blue, a *Plebejus* blue, has an extra row of black spots near the forewing margin. Other *Plebejus* blues can be recognized by the combination of an orange band on the hindwing underside, with blue-green iridescent spots but no "points" where the veins cross the marginal line, and include Acmon, Greenish, Lupine, San Emigdio, Shasta, and Veined blues.

WHERE THEY LIVE: A wide variety of open habitats.

WHAT THE CATERPILLARS EAT: Mostly legumes, with Arrowhead and Boisduval's Blues restricted to lupines. Some species eat buckwheats.

WHAT THE ADULTS EAT: Nectar. Moisture at mudpuddles.

GARDENING SUGGESTIONS: For Silvery Blue, try various vetches.

ABUNDANCE: Arrowhead and Silvery Blue are uncommon, but Silvery Blue is spreading

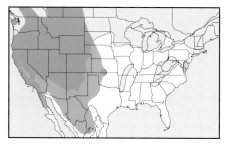

in the Northeast. They have one flight in the spring. Boisduval's and Acmon Blue are often common. Most *Plebejus* blues have one flight per year, but Acmon Blues fly throughout the warmer months.

⬤ Range of "silvery" blues.
⬤ Range of *Plebejus* blues.
⬤ Range where both are found.

Opposite: Mudpuddling male Boisduval's Blues, a species of *Plebejus* blue. ***Above:*** Arrowhead Blue.
Above inset: Acmon Blue male, a *Plebejus* blue.

"Melissa and Northern" & Sonoran Blues

No. of species: 2 + 1

LENGTH OF FOREWING: ━━━━━

HOW TO KNOW THEM: Recognize "Melissa" blues by the underside hindwing combination of orange band, blue-green iridescent spots, and black "points" where the veins intersect the marginal line. Sonoran Blues, with their gaudy orange forewing spots, are unmistakable. The two species of "melissa" blues, Melissa and Northern blues, are extremely similar in appearance.

WHERE THEY LIVE: "Melissa" blues live in a wide variety of areas, including agricultural land, disturbed areas, prairies, mountain meadows, and barrens. Sonoran Blues inhabit desert canyons where their foodplant grows.

WHAT THE CATERPILLARS EAT: "Melissa" blues eat legumes, especially lupines. Sonoran Blues eat canyon dudleya and other dudleyas.

WHAT THE ADULTS EAT: Nectar.

GARDENING SUGGESTIONS: Unlikely in your garden.

ABUNDANCE: Melissa Blues are often common in the West, rare to uncommon in the East. Most populations have two flights, from May to early September. Sonoran Blues are usually uncommon, flying in early spring.

ETC.: The eastern subspecies of Melissa Blue, 'Karner' Melissa Blue, is listed as federally endangered.

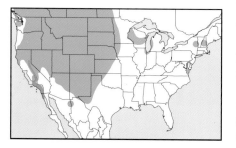

● Range of Sonoran Blue.
● Range of "Melissa and Northern" blues.
● Range where both are found.

Opposite: A pair of mated Melissa Blues — the female is somewhat larger. **Above:** Sonoran Blue male.
Above inset: Sonoran Blue female.

Scintillant Metalmarks No. of species: 8

LENGTH OF FOREWING: ──────

HOW TO KNOW THEM: Scintillant metalmarks, with their bright metallic bands and glowing green eyes, live up to their name.

WHERE THEY LIVE: Varied. Little Metalmark in open pine flats; Swamp Metalmark in wet meadows; Northern Metalmark in limestone glades; Fatal Metalmark in thorn scrub; Wright's Metalmark in desert washes and canyons.

WHAT THE CATERPILLARS EAT: Varied, depending upon species: Wright's Metalmark, sweetbush; Arizona Metalmark, Bidens; Fatal Metalmark, seepwillow and clematis; Rawson's and Rounded Metalmark, mistflowers; Little Metalmark, yellow thistle; Swamp Metalmark, swamp thistle; Northern Metalmark, round-leaved ragwort.

WHAT THE ADULTS EAT: Nectar.

GARDENING SUGGESTIONS: Not too likely in your garden, but if you live within the range of one of the species, you could try the foodplant indicated.

ABUNDANCE: Mainly rare to uncommon. The southwestern and southeastern species fly throughout the warmer months but populations farther north fly only in midsummer.

ETC.: Swamp Metalmarks are on a downward trajectory.

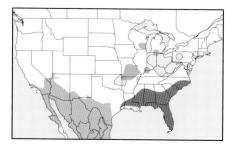

Range of Northern Metalmark.
Range of Swamp Metalmark.
Range where both are found.
Range of Little Metalmark.
Range of other scintillant metalmarks.

Opposite: Rounded Metalmark. *Above:* A Swamp Metalmark nectaring at black-eyed Susan.

Checkered Metalmarks   No. of species: 3

LENGTH OF FOREWING: ━━━━━

HOW TO KNOW THEM: Checkered metalmarks have a rather checkered appearance both above and below. And, of course, there are those green eyes.

WHERE THEY LIVE: Mormon and Palmer's Metalmark live in arid regions while Nais Metalmark inhabits openings in mountain pine forests.

WHAT THE CATERPILLARS EAT: Buckwheats for Mormon Metalmark, ceanothus for Nais Metalmark, mesquites for Palmer's Metalmark.

WHAT THE ADULTS EAT: Nectar.

GARDENING SUGGESTIONS: Not too likely to be in your garden, but buckwheats and ceanothus are great for lots of other butterflies, too, so why not try planting some?

ABUNDANCE: Mormon Metalmark, the most widespread species, is usually uncommon. Nais, found only in parts of Colorado, New Mexico, and Arizona, and Palmer's Metalmarks, from southern California to west Texas, are often common in their more restricted ranges.

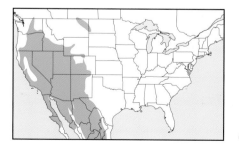

● **Range of checkered metalmarks.**

Opposite: A Nais Metalmark nectaring at ceanothus. ***Above:*** A Mormon Metalmark nectaring at Apache plume.

American Snout   No. of species: 1

LENGTH OF FOREWING: ━━━━━━━

HOW TO KNOW THEM: Read this butterfly's name. Then take a good look at the "face" of this butterfly for instant identification. The hindwing underside pattern is very variable, from unmarked pale gray, to unmarked dark gray, to highly mottled.

WHERE THEY LIVE: Usually in thickets and open woodlands, but they can be found anyplace there are hackberry trees, including suburban and urban gardens.

WHAT THE CATERPILLARS EAT: Hackberries.

WHAT THE ADULTS EAT: Nectar.

GARDENING SUGGESTIONS: Plant a hackberry and the American Snout will come.

ABUNDANCE: At the northern edges of its range, this species can be scarce. But, at times in the Southwest, there are so many *millions* of American Snouts that the accumulation of their dead bodies on the road, hit by cars, makes the roads so slick that they must be closed for safety. Almost every year, in the fall, the incredible numbers of this species makes flowering vines seem to vibrate, creating a thrilling spectacle. Sometimes, huge numbers undertake a migration. When they do, one can see them churning through the air, up as high as one can see with powerful binoculars — certainly many are flying more than 100 feet above the ground.

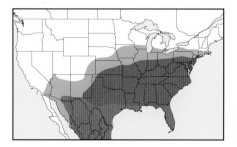

● **Range of American Snout, 1 flight.**
◑ **Range of American Snout, 2 flights.**
● **Range of American Snout, 3 flights.**

Opposite: American Snout. ***Above:*** An American Snout shares a black-eyed Susan with a beetle.

Gulf Fritillary No. of species: 1

LENGTH OF FOREWING: ━━━━━━━━━━━━━

HOW TO KNOW THEM: Gulf Fritillaries are large, orange butterflies with brightly silvered spots on their underwings. Greater fritillaries are similar but lack the red and white body stripes and the white spots at the base of the forewing topside.

WHERE THEY LIVE: Gardens, open scrub, and open woodlands.

WHAT THE CATERPILLARS EAT: Passion vines.

WHAT THE ADULTS EAT: Nectar.

GARDENING SUGGESTIONS: Very likely to be in your garden. Plant passion vines, including the southeastern natives, corky-stemmed passion vine and maypop, or the Texas native, Tagua passion vine. In southern California, where there are no native passion vines, Gulf Fritillaries use blue passion vines and other ornamental species.

ABUNDANCE: Common to abundant, flying throughout the warmer months in the South, becoming a late-summer immigrant farther north.

ETC.: How fortunate we are that such a sensational butterfly is so common and wide-spread. Gulf Fritillaries are so dazzling on both their topside and underside that no matter how many one sees, one wants to see another. Like Piperine Swallowtail, this butterfly will benefit greatly from the explosive growth of butterfly gardening.

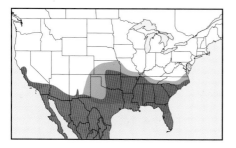

🔘 **Range of Gulf Fritillary, 1 flight.**
🔘 **Range of Gulf Fritillary, 2 flights.**
🔘 **Range of Gulf Fritillary, 3 flights.**

Opposite: A Gulf Fritillary nectaring at thistle. *Above:* A Gulf Fritillary nectaring at lantana. *Above inset:* A Gulf Fritillary caterpillar on its foodplant, passion vine.

Heliconians   No. of species: 2

LENGTH OF FOREWING: ━━━━━━━━━━

HOW TO KNOW THEM: With their bold black and yellow coloration, Zebra Heliconians are unmistakable. Julia Heliconians have the same unusually narrow wing shape, but are bright orange. Both fly with shallow wingbeats, but the flight of Zebra Heliconians is much more languid and floating than is that of Julia Heliconians.

WHERE THEY LIVE: Gardens, open woodlands, and disturbed open areas.

WHAT THE CATERPILLARS EAT: Passion vines.

WHAT THE ADULTS EAT: Nectar.

GARDENING SUGGESTIONS: Very likely to be in your garden. Plant passion vines, including southeastern natives corky-stemmed passion vine and maypop, or the Texas native, Tagua passion vine.

ABUNDANCE: Common to abundant, flying throughout the warmer months in southern Florida and Texas, emigrating northward as summer progresses.

ETC.: Zebra Heliconians often come together at night to form clustered roosts. Heliconians are among the longest-lived butterflies in the world, with a lifespan of about nine months. Another three species of Heliconians have been known to stray into southern Texas from Mexico.

● **Range where both Zebra and Julia Heliconians are found.**
● **Range of Zebra Heliconians.**

Opposite: A Julia Heliconian nectaring at Spanish needles. *Top:* Zebra Heliconian at lantana. *Bottom:* Zebra Heliconian at zinnia. *Bottom inset:* Zebra Heliconian caterpillars.

Greater Fritillaries   No. of species: 14

LENGTH OF FOREWING: ━━━━━━━━━━━━━━

HOW TO KNOW THEM: Greater fritillaries are big, bold, and beautiful. Examples are shown above and on the next three pages. All have the same general design: brown-orange above with black markings and a yellow/brown underside with large pale spots that are usually silvered. Many of the species are so similar that the identity of individual butterflies is often debated by even experienced butterfly enthusiasts. Species include Aphrodite, Atlantis, Callippe, Coronis, Diana, Edwards', Great Basin, Great Spangled, Hydaspe, Mormon, Nokomis, Regal, Unsilvered, and Zerene fritillaries.

WHERE THEY LIVE: Woodland openings, meadows, prairies, and other open habitats where violets are found.

WHAT THE CATERPILLARS EAT: Violets.

WHAT THE ADULTS EAT: Nectar.

GARDENING SUGGESTIONS: Likely to be in your garden. Plant violets.

ABUNDANCE: Many of the species can be common to abundant, with one long flight period — mainly June–August. Great Spangled Fritillary is the most common eastern species and also ranges throughout the West. In contrast, Unsilvered Fritillary, flying in just a few localities near the California coast, is range-restricted and rare and needs to be protected.

Range of greater fritillaries.

Opposite: A Mormon Fritillary nectaring at fleabane. ***Above:*** A Great Spangled Fritillary female nectaring at zinnia.

Greater Fritillaries *(continued)*

LENGTH OF FOREWING: ━━━━━━━━━━━

HOW TO KNOW THEM: The two magnificent species shown above and on the opposite page deviate, to some extent, from the greater fritillary pattern. Diana Fritillaries are two-toned, the males orange and very dark brown, the females pale blue and blue-black. The very clean hindwing pattern of Nokomis Fritillary can vary from buff yellow, as shown, to yellow and brown, to buff and blue.

WHERE THEY LIVE: Diana Fritillaries dwell in glades within moist mountain forests. Nokomis Fritillaries inhabit wet meadows in arid country.

WHAT THE CATERPILLARS EAT: Violets.

WHAT THE ADULTS EAT: Nectar.

GARDENING SUGGESTIONS: These two species are unlikely to be in your garden.

ABUNDANCE: Both of the species shown above and on the opposite page are rare to uncommon. Diana flies mainly July–September, Nokomis mainly August–September.

ETC.: Similarly to most greater fritillaries, males of these two species emerge before females, who then fly later in the season.

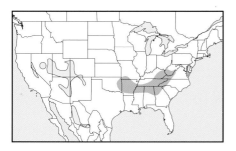

● Range of Nokomis Fritillary.
● Range of Diana Fritillary.

Opposite: A male Diana Fritillary obtaining salts from gravel. ***Above:*** A Nokomis Fritillary nectaring at thistle.

Lesser Fritillaries No. of species: 12

LENGTH OF FOREWING: ━━━━━━━━━

HOW TO KNOW THEM: Lesser fritillaries look like small versions of greater fritillaries. The typical pattern of most species is very similar to that of the species shown on these pages. On the underside of the hindwing, many species have a duck-head pattern, with a black "eye" near the wing base, followed by a white "bill." Species include Alberta, Astarte, Bog, Dingy, Freija, Frigga, Meadow, Mountain, Pacific, Purplish, Relict, and Silver-bordered fritillaries.

WHERE THEY LIVE: Mainly in wet meadows and bogs, with some species specifically in willow bogs.

WHAT THE CATERPILLARS EAT: Violets, willows, blueberries and relatives.

WHAT THE ADULTS EAT: Nectar.

GARDENING SUGGESTIONS: Unlikely to be in your garden.

ABUNDANCE: Most species are uncommon, but both Pacific Fritillary (in moist forest openings in the Pacific Northwest) and Meadow Fritillary (in more open meadows and field of the Northeast) can be quite common.

Range of lesser fritillaries.

Opposite: Purplish Fritillary (so named for the purplish tones on its underside). ***Above:*** A Silver-bordered Fritillary nectaring at bluets.

Patches   No. of species: 5

LENGTH OF FOREWING: ━━━━━━━━

HOW TO KNOW THEM: On their topsides, all five North American species normally have white spots on the forewings and an orange or red-orange patch on the hindwings. On the undersides, all five have the black patch on the hindwing containing a row of white spots. Species include Banded, Bordered, California, Crimson, and Definite patches.

WHERE THEY LIVE: Mainly in tropical and subtropical thorn scrub.

WHAT THE CATERPILLARS EAT: Mainly sunflowers, but some of the less common species, including Crimson Patch, eat plants in the acanthus family.

WHAT THE ADULTS EAT: Nectar.

GARDENING SUGGESTIONS: Sunflowers.

ABUNDANCE: Bordered Patch is common from southern Texas west to southeastern Arizona, flying throughout warm weather. California Patch can be common in southeastern California in March and April.

ETC.: This group of exotic butterflies is subtropical and tropical and, in the United States, is encountered mainly along the Mexican border.

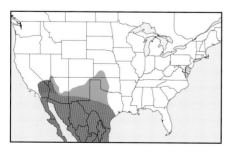

● **Range of patches, 1 flight.**
● **Range of patches, 2 flights.**
● **Range of patches, 3 flights.**

Opposite: A Bordered Patch nectaring at mistflower. ***Opposite inset:*** Bordered Patch caterpillar.
Above: Crimson Patches nectaring at mistflower.

Checkerspots No. of species: 21

LENGTH OF FOREWING: ▬▬▬▬▬▬

HOW TO KNOW THEM: Almost all of these medium-sized butterflies have striking rows of orange and white alternating on the underside of the hindwing. Examples are shown above and on the next five pages. On their topsides, most species are orange and black and usually have the appearance of a "face" on their hindwings (with an "eye" at the base of each hindwing and the abdomen as the "nose"). Species include Arachne, Baltimore, Black, Chinati, Dotted, Edith's, Elada, Fulvia, Gabb's, Gillett's, Gorgone, Harris', Hoffmann's, Leanira, Northern, Rockslide, Sagebrush, Silvery, Theona, Tiny, and Variable checkerspots.

WHERE THEY LIVE: In many different habitats, depending upon the species.

WHAT THE CATERPILLARS EAT: Most eat aster family plants, especially asters and sunflowers, some eat acanthus family plants while some eat beardtongues. Some species will eat only one plant species—for example, Harris' Checkerspots will eat only flat-topped white asters.

WHAT THE ADULTS EAT: Nectar.

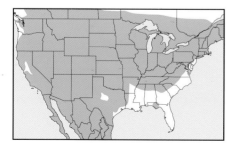

GARDENING SUGGESTIONS: Sunflowers.

ABUNDANCE: Mostly uncommon, but Gorgone Checkerspot, in the prairie province, as well as some of the other species, can be common.

● **Range of checkerspots.**

Opposite: Sagebrush Checkerspot. *Above:* A Harris' Checkerspot at blue flag. *Above inset:* Harris' Checkerspot caterpillar has the same colors as the adult.

Checkerspots *(continued)*

LENGTH OF FOREWING: ━━━━━━━━

HOW TO KNOW THEM: The five species of *Thessalia* checkerspots—Black, Chinati, Fulvia, Leanira, and Theona—are closely related to one another taxonomically and share similar patterns. The underside of the hindwing has white bands alternating with either black or orange bands. Above, there is a prominent white spot in the middle of the crown of the head.

WHERE THEY LIVE: *Thessalia* checkerspots live mainly in arid open country, including open pine woodlands, sagebrush steppes, grasslands, and sand dunes.

WHAT THE CATERPILLARS EAT: Mainly Indian paintbrushes, but in Texas, Theona Checkerspots prefer silverleafs.

WHAT THE ADULTS EAT: Nectar.

GARDENING SUGGESTIONS: Caterpillars are not likely to be in your garden, but adults will come to a wide variety of good nectar sources.

ABUNDANCE: Mostly uncommon. None of the species is really widespread. Leanira Checkerspot can be found in most of California and Nevada; Fulvia Checkerspot

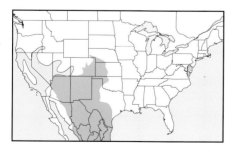

in most of Arizona and New Mexico. Theona Checkerspot occurs mainly along the Mexican border, from central Arizona to extreme southern Texas.

● **Range of Leanira Checkerspot.**
● **Range of Theona, Chinati, Fulvia, and Black checkerspots.**

Opposite: Leanira Checkerspot. *Above:* Theona Checkerspot. *Above inset:* Theona Checkerspot.

Checkerspots (continued)

LENGTH OF FOREWING: ━━━━━━━

HOW TO KNOW THEM: The four *Euphydryas* checkerspots—Variable, Baltimore, Edith's, and Gillett's checkerspots—are especially closely related to one another taxonomically and are particularly dazzling. Most individuals have antennal clubs that are luminous yellow. Variable and Edith's Checkerspots are often indistinguishable in the field.

WHERE THEY LIVE: In many different habitats, depending upon the species.

WHAT THE CATERPILLARS EAT: Variable Checkerspots eat a variety of plants, including beard tongues, Indian paintbrushes, and snowberries. Baltimore Checkerspots usually eat turtlehead. Edith's Checkerspots eat Indian paintbrushes, Chinese-houses, and others. Gillett's Checkerspots eat twinberry honeysuckle.

WHAT THE ADULTS EAT: Nectar.

GARDENING SUGGESTIONS: Turtlehead, beard tongues.

ABUNDANCE: Variable Checkerspot is often common to abundant. Baltimore Checkerspot is usually uncommon but can become common in some areas. Edith's and Gillett's Checkerspots are mainly rare to uncommon. All have one flight per year.

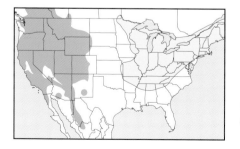

Range of Baltimore Checkerspot.
Range of Variable, Edith's, and Gillett's checkerspots.

Opposite: A Variable Checkerspot nectaring at downy cologania. *Above:* A Baltimore Checkerspot nectaring at an orange milkweed. *Above inset:* Baltimore Checkerspot caterpillar.

Crescents   No. of species: 13

LENGTH OF FOREWING: ▬▬▬▬

HOW TO KNOW THEM: Crescents are small versions of fritillaries, flying on stiff wings with shallow wingbeats. Examples are shown above and on the next three pages. Unlike the fritillaries, they have only a partial, vertical row of black spots on the forewing topside. Species include California, Cuban, Field, Mylitta, Northern, Painted, Pale, Pale-banded, Phaon, Pearl, Tawny, Texan, and Vesta crescents.

WHERE THEY LIVE: In many different habitats, depending upon the species.

WHAT THE CATERPILLARS EAT: Pearl Crescents, Field Crescents, and their relatives eat asters. Another group of western species eat thistles. Other species use other plants.

WHAT THE ADULTS EAT: Nectar.

GARDENING SUGGESTIONS: Very possible in your garden if you plant asters.

ABUNDANCE: A number of the widespread species, including Field Crescent and Pearl Crescent, are common to abundant, flying throughout warm weather. Pearl Crescents are the only crescents found in many areas (I have included the range of Northern Crescents with that of Pearl Crescents, as it is likely that the two are best treated as one species.).

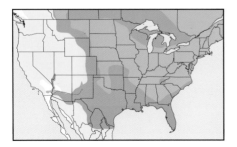

○ **Range where crescents other than Pearl Crescents are found.**

● **Range where both Pearl and other crescents occur.**

● **Range of Pearl Crescents.**

Opposite: A Field Crescent nectaring at leafy-headed aster. *Above:* A Pearl Crescent nectaring at black-eyed Susan.

Crescents (continued)

LENGTH OF FOREWING: ━━━━━━

HOW TO KNOW THEM: Most crescents look very similar to the Pearl Crescent shown on the previous page, but the two shown here are different. Texan Crescents stand out in particular: they are redder, with wide black borders and with off-white spot bands on the hindwings. Phaon Crescents are more cream-colored below than are other crescents, with a bold cream-colored patch on the forewing.

WHERE THEY LIVE: Phaon Crescents are found in moist, open areas. Texan Crescents prefer brushier situations.

WHAT THE CATERPILLARS EAT: Phaon Crescents eat fogfruit. Texan Crescents use acanthus family plants.

WHAT THE ADULTS EAT: Nectar.

GARDENING SUGGESTIONS: Likely to be in your garden. Plant fogfruit for Phaons, shrimp plants and ruellias for Texans.

ABUNDANCE: Phaon Crescents are usually common and can be abundant. Texan Crescents are common westward, rare to uncommon eastward. Both species fly throughout the warmer months.

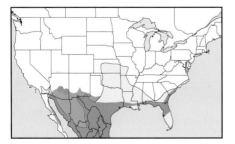

ETC.: One can often encounter Texan Crescents while walking along man-made paths through woodlands, because the males love to patrol along these paths.

○ **Range of Phaon Crescent.**
● **Range of Texan Crescent.**
● **Range where both are found.**

Opposite: A Phaon Crescent nectaring at fogfruit, its caterpillar foodplant. *Above:* A Texan Crescent nectaring at lantana.

Anglewings   No. of species: 7

LENGTH OF FOREWING: ━━━━━━━━━━━━

HOW TO KNOW THEM: The wing margins of anglewings, medium-sized butterflies, are very ragged and angled. On the underside, in the center of the hindwing, is a punctuation mark—either a comma or a question mark. Species include Question Mark, as well as Eastern, Gray, Green, Hoary, Oreas, and Satyr commas.

WHERE THEY LIVE: Anglewings are usually true woodland butterflies, although Question Marks can survive in suburbia.

WHAT THE CATERPILLARS EAT: A variety of trees, including hackberries, elms, and willows. Also nettles and, for some species, currants, and gooseberries.

WHAT THE ADULTS EAT: Tree sap, rotting fruit and other decaying organic matter. Moisture at mudpuddles, damp sand, and soil. Rarely do they visit flowers.

GARDENING SUGGESTIONS: Possible in your garden. Plant hackberries or elms in the East. Try currants in the West.

ABUNDANCE: Although widespread, one usually does not see many at one time.

ETC.: Walking along dirt roads through woodlands, one is likely to encounter these sylvan spirits as they obtain salts from the roadway soil. Anglewings are some of the only North American butterflies to overwinter as adults, crawling into cracks in trees or man-made structures.

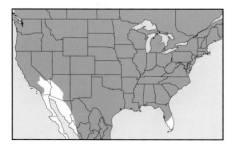

● **Range of anglewings.**

All the butterflies shown here are obtaining salts from damp sand. **Opposite:** Hoary Comma. **Top:** Green Comma. **Bottom:** Question Mark. **Bottom inset:** Question Mark caterpillar.

Tortoiseshells   No. of species: 4

LENGTH OF FOREWING: ━━━━━━━━━

HOW TO KNOW THEM: Tortoiseshells are closely related to anglewings and look much like them below — but without quite so prominent a comma. Above, there is nothing like a Mourning Cloak, with its plush brown velvety color, studded with royal blue and edged in ochre. The three other North American species have whitish spots near the forewing apex.

WHERE THEY LIVE: These are butterflies of woodlands — most at home in the forest.

WHAT THE CATERPILLARS EAT: Mourning Cloaks and Compton Tortoiseshells eat willows and birches. California Tortoiseshells eat ceanothus while Milbert's Tortoiseshells eat nettles.

WHAT THE ADULTS EAT: Tree sap, rotting fruit, and other decaying organic matter. Moisture at soil and gravel. Rarely do they visit flowers.

GARDENING SUGGESTIONS: Possible in your garden. Plant shrubby willows, small birches, and ceanothus.

ABUNDANCE: Mainly uncommon to common, flying throughout warm weather. California Tortoiseshell periodically undergoes huge population explosions. **ETC.:** Mourning Cloaks migrate southward for the winter, but very little is known about these movements.

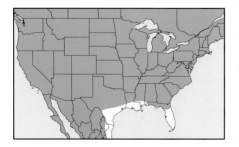

● **Range of tortoiseshells.**

Opposite: A Mourning Cloak at damp sand. *Top left:* A Compton Tortoiseshell at damp sand.
Top right: California Tortoiseshell caterpillars. *Bottom:* Milbert's Tortoiseshell.

Ladies No. of species: 4

LENGTH OF FOREWING: ━━━━━━━━━━

HOW TO KNOW THEM: Ladies are medium-sized butterflies whose wing shape and rapid and nervous flight differ greatly from other orange fliers, such as fritillaries and crescents. The cobweb pattern on the undersides of their hindwings is unique. All four species are shown on this and the following three pages.

WHERE THEY LIVE: Extremely wide-ranging in open areas.

WHAT THE CATERPILLARS EAT: Painted Ladies eat thistles and other plants. American Ladies eat pearly-everlastings, cudweeds, and other aster-family plants.

WHAT THE ADULTS EAT: Nectar.

GARDENING SUGGESTIONS: Very likely in your garden. Plant thistles for Painted Ladies; pearly everlastings, pussytoes, and cudweeds for American Ladies.

ABUNDANCE: Luckily, ladies are everywhere! They are mainly common to abundant, although numbers vary greatly from year to year. All species fly throughout warm weather.

ETC.: Painted Ladies are the most widespread butterfly on Earth, living on five continents. Ladies cannot survive freezing temperatures. Each year, Painted Ladies stream northward from their north Mexico strongholds, often in numbers so impressive that everyone notices, to repopulate much of North America.

● **Range of ladies.**

Opposite: A Painted Lady nectaring at an azalea, a rarely used plant. ***Above:*** An American Lady nectaring at Canada thistle. ***Above inset:*** American Lady caterpillar.

Ladies (continued)

LENGTH OF FOREWING: ────────────

HOW TO KNOW THEM: West Coast Lady is very similar to Painted and American Ladies, but the fourth lady, the Red Admiral, is sailing on a different ship. Those bright red-orange forewing stripes accord the privileges of rank.

WHERE THEY LIVE: Many types of open areas. Red Admirals seem to be especially comfortable in moist situations.

WHAT THE CATERPILLARS EAT: West Coast Ladies eat mallow family plants. Red Admirals eat nettles and relatives.

WHAT THE ADULTS EAT: All species nectar at flowers. Red Admirals also frequently obtain nutrients from sap, rotting fruit, decaying organic matter and scat.

GARDENING SUGGESTIONS: Possible in your garden. Plant mallows for West Coast Lady. For Red Admirals, try pellitory and false nettle rather than nettles, which can be a nuisance in the garden.

ABUNDANCE: Mostly uncommon, but Red Admirals occasionally have tremendous population explosions and northward emigrations. All species fly throughout warm weather.

ETC.: The "misnamed" Red Admiral is actually a lady, not an admiral. Some believe that the original name given to the butterfly in England (where it also flies) was Red Admirable, which was subsequently corrupted to Red Admiral.

● **Range of ladies.**

Opposite: West Coast Lady. *Above:* Red Admiral.

Buckeyes   No. of species: 3

LENGTH OF FOREWING: ━━━━━━━━

HOW TO KNOW THEM: Buckeyes are medium-sized, brown brushfoots. Look for the big eye-spots, on the forewings and hindwings, on the underwings and the topsides — they're everywhere!

WHERE THEY LIVE: A variety of open habitats, including brushy fields, disturbed areas, coastal dunes, and scrub. Mangrove Buckeyes are restricted to edges of black mangrove swamps and adjacent areas.

WHAT THE CATERPILLARS EAT: Common Buckeyes eat fogfruits, gerardias, plantain, monkey flowers, and others. Mangrove Buckeyes eat black mangrove. Tropical Buckeyes eat fogfruits, ruellias, and others.

WHAT THE ADULTS EAT: Nectar.

GARDENING SUGGESTIONS: Very possible in your garden. Plant fogfruits, monkey flowers, and snapdragons.

ABUNDANCE: Common to abundant southward, Common Buckeyes move northward as the season progresses. Usually scarce to uncommon in the northern reaches of their range, they occasionally become common there as well. Mangrove and Tropical Buckeyes are generally rare to uncommon.

ETC.: Buckeyes love to perch on bare ground, and so they are more likely on a path than off of it.

● **Range of Common Buckeyes**
● **Range where both Common Buckeyes and other buckeyes occur.**

Opposite: A Common Buckeye nectaring at ox-eyed daisy. **Above:** A Common Buckeye nectaring at joe-pye weed.

Peacocks   No. of species: I

LENGTH OF FOREWING: ━━━━━━━━━━

HOW TO KNOW THEM: They don't strut, but they are showy! White Peacocks are silvery white with an orange hindwing border. Below, they have beautiful red-orange markings. They fly low to the ground on shallow wingbeats.

WHERE THEY LIVE: Moist, open habitats.

WHAT THE CATERPILLARS EAT: Bacopas, fogfruits, ruellias, and other plants in the snapdragon, acanthus, and verbena families.

WHAT THE ADULTS EAT: Nectar.

GARDENING SUGGESTIONS: Very possible in your garden. Plant smooth water hyssop and green shrimp plant.

ABUNDANCE: Common to abundant in the southern part of its range. An immigrant northward, decreasing in abundance to the north. Flight is throughout the warmer months.

ETC.: The populations in Florida and Texas look slightly different from one another, though they are the same species: the Texas butterflies often have a smoky tone, while the Florida butterflies have more orange on their topsides. Another peacock, Banded Peacock, is a rare stray from Mexico to the Lower Rio Grande Valley of Texas.

● **Range of White Peacocks.**

Opposite: A White Peacock nectaring at mistflower. *Above:* White Peacock.

Malachite & Daggerwings   No. of species: 1 + 2

LENGTH OF FOREWING: ─────────────────

HOW TO KNOW THEM: Malachites are the unmistakable big green machines of the butterfly world. Daggerwings have a very distinctive wing shape, especially the hindwing dagger-tail. Ruddy Daggerwing is bright red-orange on the topside.

WHERE THEY LIVE: Tropical hammocks.

WHAT THE CATERPILLARS EAT: Malachites eat green shrimp plants, ruellias, and others. Daggerwings eat figs.

WHAT THE ADULTS EAT: Nectar and rotting fruits.

GARDENING SUGGESTIONS: Very possible in your garden in south Florida and extreme southern Texas. For Malachites, plant green shrimp plant or ruellias. For daggerwings, plant figs, for example, short-leaf fig.

ABUNDANCE: Malachite is uncommon, flying throughout the year. Ruddy Daggerwing is uncommon to common in south Florida. Both Ruddy and Many-banded Daggerwings are rare in extreme southern Texas. Flight is throughout the year.

ETC.: Malachite belongs to the true brushfoots subfamily while daggerwings belong to the admirals and relatives subfamily.

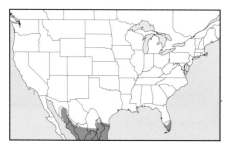

○ **Range of daggerwings.**

● **Range where both daggerwings and Malachite occur.**

● **Range of Malachite.**

Opposite: Ruddy Daggerwing. ***Above:*** Malachite.

Admirals   No. of species: 4

LENGTH OF FOREWING: ━━━━━━━━━━━━━━

HOW TO KNOW THEM: North American admirals come in three striking color patterns, making identification easy. All patterns are shown on this and the next three pages. The first pattern is that of the Red-spotted Purple, a subspecies of Red-spotted Admiral. With its brilliant blue colors and red spots, it could only be confused with Pipevine Swallowtail, but it doesn't have tails. The second pattern is that of Lorquin's Admiral (shown on page 160), Weidemeyer's Admiral, and White Admiral, with a broad white stripe on a dark background. The third pattern, featuring orange and black, is shown on page 161.

WHERE THEY LIVE: Moist woodlands, including many suburban areas.

WHAT THE CATERPILLARS EAT: Cherries, poplars, birches, and other trees.

WHAT THE ADULTS EAT: Mainly decaying organic matter, rotting fruit, and scat; moisture at damp sand.

GARDENING SUGGESTIONS: Red-spotted Admirals are possible in your garden. Try planting small wild cherries and birches.

ABUNDANCE: Uncommon to common, depending upon location. Flies throughout warmer months southward, June–August northward.

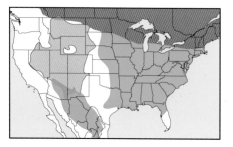

○ Range of Weidemeyer's Admiral.

● Range of Red-spotted Purple.

● Range where both Weidemeyer's and Red-spotted Admirals are found.

◐ Range of White Admiral.

Opposite and above: Red-spotted Purple, which, along with White Admiral, is a subspecies of Red-spotted Admiral.

Admirals *(continued)*

LENGTH OF FOREWING: ━━━━━━━━━━━━━━

HOW TO KNOW THEM: Northern populations of Red-spotted Admiral have a broad white stripe across the wings as do Lorquin's and Weidemeyer's Admirals. Viceroys, presumably mimicking Monarchs, look completely different and are bright orange. They can be differentiated from Monarchs by their smaller size, the presence of a black line in the middle of the hindwing, and most easily, by their gliding flight, on flat wings, compared to Monarchs' flight, on V-shaped wings.

WHERE THEY LIVE: Moist woodlands and riparian areas for Lorquin's and Weidemeyer's Admirals; moist open areas with shrubby willows for Viceroys.

WHAT THE CATERPILLARS EAT: Viceroys eat only willows; Lorquin's and Weidemeyer's Admirals will also eat poplars, aspens, and other trees.

WHAT THE ADULTS EAT: Nectar.

GARDENING SUGGESTIONS: Unlikely to be in your garden.

ABUNDANCE: Uncommon to common.

ETC.: Males love to perch in shrubs or low trees and patrol short stretches of trails and roadways. In the South, Viceroys are darker orange-brown, more closely resembling Queens, which are close relatives of Monarchs.

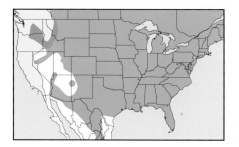

● **Range of Lorquin's Admiral.**
● **Range of Viceroy.**
● **Range where both are found.**

Opposite: A Lorquin's Admiral nectaring at coyote mint. ***Above:*** A Viceroy nectaring at white-bracted thoroughwort. ***Above inset:*** Viceroy caterpillar.

Leafwings No. of species: 3

LENGTH OF FOREWING: ━━━━━━━━━━━

HOW TO KNOW THEM: The first member of the group that espied the butterfly shown on the opposite page exclaimed, "Get over here, there's an incredible leafwing…uh oh, my mistake, it actually is a leaf!" Of course, it was a butterfly. The three species are quite similar, with mottled gray-brown underwings. They rarely show off their bright reddish-brown topsides.

WHAT THE CATERPILLARS EAT: Crotons, with Florida Leafwing eating only narrow-leaved croton.

WHAT THE ADULTS EAT: Rotting fruit, decaying organic matter.

GARDENING SUGGESTIONS: Unlikely in your garden, but you could try planting crotons.

ABUNDANCE: Although locally common in parts of their range, these butterflies are mainly rare to uncommon. Flight is through much of the year.

ETC.: Goatweed Leafwing is one of the few species to overwinter as an adult. A few Mexican species occasionally stray into the Lower Rio Grande Valley of Texas. The Mexican species shown on the opposite page illustrates just how realistically some leafwings mimic leaves. The fact that each individual is slightly different makes the camouflage all the more successful.

 Range of Goatweed Leafwing.
 Range of Tropical Leafwing.
 Range where both Goatweed and Tropical leafwing are found.
 Range of Florida Leafwing.

Opposite left: Tropical Leafwing. ***Opposite right:*** A Florida Leafwing laying an egg on narrow-leaved croton. ***Above:*** A Holey Leafwing, a Mexican species, comes to fruit bait. ***Above inset:*** Tropical Leafwing caterpillar.

Emperors No. of species: 3

LENGTH OF FOREWING: ━━━━━━━━━━━

HOW TO KNOW THEM: All three North American species have warm brown topsides with a row of prominent black eye-spots along the hindwing border. Males have more angular wings and more black at the forewing apex than do females.

WHERE THEY LIVE: Anyplace with hackberries.

WHAT THE CATERPILLARS EAT: Hackberries.

WHAT THE ADULTS EAT: Mainly sap and rotting fruit.

GARDENING SUGGESTIONS: Very likely to be in your garden. Plant hackberries and you will be rewarded.

ABUNDANCE: Mainly uncommon to common, but often abundant in southern Texas and some other areas. Hackberry Emperors and Tawny Emperors are the most widespread. Empress Leilias are restricted to the area from southern Texas through central Arizona. Found throughout the warmer months.

ETC.: Emperors show no fear. They readily land on people's hats, clothing, and fingers, looking for all that good salt that is in human perspiration. Some really lucky (and sweaty) butterfliers have had all three species of emperors land on them at the same time. In addition to the three North American species, an additional three species of emperors occasionally stray into extreme south Texas and southeastern Arizona.

● **Range of emperors.**

Opposite: A Tawny Emperor probes a human finger for salt with its tongue. *Above:* Empress Leilia.
Above inset: Empress Leilia caterpillar.

Pearly-eyes & Browns   No. of species: 3 + 2

LENGTH OF FOREWING: ————————

HOW TO KNOW THEM: All the pearly-eyes and browns are brown, medium-sized butterflies with a group of four to five eye-spots near the hindwing border and a larger eye-spot near the hindwing leading margin. Pearly-eyes have the hindwing spots surrounded *as a group* with white, while browns have a white circle around *each* eye-spot. Species of pearly-eyes include Creole, Northern, and Southern pearly-eyes; browns include Appalachian and Eyed browns.

WHERE THEY LIVE: Most species live in woodlands, especially wet woodlands, but Eyed Browns inhabit wet meadows and marshes.

WHAT THE CATERPILLARS EAT: Pearly-eyes eat canes and other grasses; browns eat sedges.

WHAT THE ADULTS EAT: Mainly tree sap and decaying organic matter. Flowers are not normally visited.

GARDENING SUGGESTIONS: Unlikely to be in your garden.

ABUNDANCE: Generally uncommon, but Eyed Browns can be abundant in some wetlands.

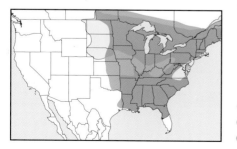

● Range of browns.
● Range of pearly-eyes.
● Range where both are found.

Opposite: Northern Pearly-eye. *Above:* Eyed Brown.

Small Satyrs   No. of species: 8

LENGTH OF FOREWING: ━━━━━━

HOW TO KNOW THEM: Small and brown, these satyrs weave through grasses with a characteristic bouncing flight pattern. Upon close inspection one group of three species, the gemmed-satyrs (including Nabokov's Satyr), has a shimmering gray-metallic patch on the hindwing that contains "gemming." Little Wood-Satyr and Carolina Satyr are the plainest species, being dull brown with a few eye-spots.

WHERE THEY LIVE: Most species favor grassy areas within woodlands or at woodland edges. Mitchell's Satyr lives in fens and boggy swamps. Its close relative, Georgia Satyr, inhabits bogs in the north, grassy pine-woods southward.

WHAT THE CATERPILLARS EAT: Most species eat grasses. Mitchell's and Georgia Satyrs use sedges.

WHAT THE ADULTS EAT: Most of these species are rarely observed eating anything.

GARDENING SUGGESTIONS: Possible in gardens, but little you can do will attract them.

ABUNDANCE: Little Wood-Satyr and Carolina Satyr are abundant in the East. Red Satyrs are abundant in the Southwest. Other species are uncommon. Mitchell's is federally endangered, with scattered populations in Michigan, North Carolina, and Virginia. Recently, my partner, Jane Scott, and I found a major population in Alabama. Gemmed Satyr is in the southeast while Canyonland Satyr is in the southwest.

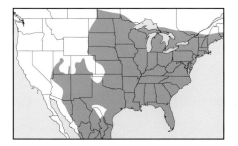

● **Range of small satyrs.**

Opposite: Mitchell's Satyr. Until recently, Mitchell's Satyr was found in Ohio and in New Jersey. The Ohio populations were lost to development and the New Jersey populations to a combination of development and the senseless killing of the butterflies by unethical butterfly collectors. These collectors returned day after day, year after year, to the few, very small fens where the butterfly was found. They illegally collected and killed these animals for their own amusement and, in some cases, profit. Toward the end, even chain-link fences, guard dogs, and a security guard could not keep the poachers out. ***Above:*** Nabokov's Satyr.

Ringlets & Wood-Nymphs   No. of species: 2 + 4

LENGTH OF FOREWING, RINGLETS: ━━━━━━━━━

LENGTH OF FOREWING, WOOD-NYMPHS: ━━━━━━━━━━━

HOW TO KNOW THEM: Across North America, the appearance of ringlets varies quite a bit. In California, they are very pale, almost white, while farther east they become dark. However, almost all of them have a characteristic jagged white band in the middle of the hindwing. Wood-nymphs are large satyrs with two bold eye-spots on the forewing, tightly ringed with yellow. In most of the East these eye-spots are surrounded by bright yellow-orange; farther west the yellow-orange patch is missing. Species of wood-nymphs include Common, Great Basin, Mead's, and Small wood-nymphs.

WHERE THEY LIVE: Open grassy areas. Hayden's Ringlet is restricted to high-elevation subalpine and alpine meadows.

WHAT THE CATERPILLARS EAT: Grasses.

WHAT THE ADULTS EAT: Nectar, though wood-nymphs nectar less often than most butterflies.

GARDENING SUGGESTIONS: Not likely in your garden.

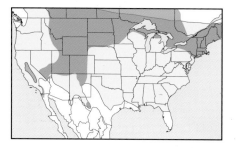

ABUNDANCE: Common Ringlets are common to abundant, with two or three flights per year. Wood-nymphs are common to abundant, with one flight — predominantly in July–August.

  Range of wood-nymphs.
  Range of ringlets.
  Range where both are found.

Opposite: Common Ringlet. *Above:* Mating Common Wood-Nymphs.

Alpines & Arctics No. of species: 6 + 9

LENGTH OF FOREWING, ALPINES: ━━━━━━━━

LENGTH OF FOREWING, ARCTICS: ━━━━━━━━━

HOW TO KNOW THEM: These are butterflies of the far north (and the "far up"). Alpines are medium-sized, and mainly dark brown with orange patches on the wings. Arctics are somewhat larger than are alpines with mottled brown wings that blend with the lichen-encrusted rocks on which they rest. The flight of alpines and arctics is more direct, less bouncy, than is that of many other satyrs. Species of alpines include Colorado, Common, Disa, Magdalena, Theano, and Vidler's. Species of arctics include Alberta, Chryxus, Great, Jutta, Macoun's, Melissa, Polixenes, Uhler's, and White-veined.

WHERE THEY LIVE: Most alpines live in alpine or subalpine meadows, but one is found exclusively on alpine rockslides. Arctics are found in a greater variety of habitats, including rocky alpine meadows, dry grasslands and grassy openings in coniferous forests.

WHAT THE CATERPILLARS EAT: Grasses and sedges.

WHAT THE ADULTS EAT: Very little, though some species occasionally visit flowers.

GARDENING SUGGESTIONS: Extremely unlikely to be in your garden.

ABUNDANCE: Of the alpines, only Common Alpine is widespread. Others are restricted to high peaks in Wyoming and Colorado and, for one species, Washington State. Arctics are mostly uncommon, but can be locally abundant. All have one flight per year or one flight every other year (it's so cold where they live that it takes two years for the caterpillar to develop into an adult).

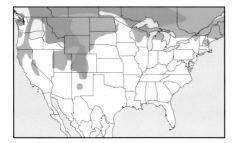

○ **Range of alpines.**

● **Range of arctics.**

● **Range where both are found.**

Opposite: Theano Alpine. ***Top left:*** Vidler's Alpine. ***Top right:*** Chryxus Arctic. ***Bottom:*** Melissa Arctic.

"Monarchs" No. of species: 3

LENGTH OF FOREWING: ━━━━━━━━━━━━━━━━━━━━━━━

HOW TO KNOW THEM: Given the tremendous publicity that Monarchs have received, many Americans identify every large butterfly that they see as a Monarch. Big and yellow with black stripes — it's a Monarch! Big and dark brown with a yellow border — it's a Monarch! But the Monarch that everyone is talking about is actually a large orange butterfly. Its veins are black and its black borders contain double rows of white dots. In flight, Monarchs often sail with their wings in a V. Viceroys are similar, but smaller, with a black band on the hindwing, and glide with their wings flat, not in a V. See the following pages for the other "monarchs," Queen and Soldier.

WHERE THEY LIVE: Open areas with milkweeds, including roadsides, gardens, grassy fields, and agricultural areas. During migration they can be anywhere, including the streets of downtown Manhattan.

WHAT THE CATERPILLARS EAT: Milkweeds.

WHAT THE ADULTS EAT: Nectar.

GARDENING SUGGESTIONS: Milkweeds.

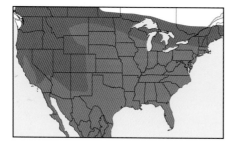

ABUNDANCE: Generally common, but numbers vary from year to year.

ETC.: See page 34 for more gardening suggestions and further information about Monarch migration.

● **Range of Monarch, 2 flights.**
● **Range of Monarch, 3 flights.**

Opposite: Monarch. ***Above:*** A Monarch nectaring at common milkweed. ***Above inset:*** Monarch caterpillar.

Monarchs (continued)

LENGTH OF FOREWING: ————————————————

HOW TO KNOW THEM: Queens and Soldiers are very similar in appearance to Monarchs, but they are clothed in more somber colors.

WHERE THEY LIVE: Open areas with milkweeds, including roadsides, gardens, thorn scrub, and open subtropical woodland.

WHAT THE CATERPILLARS EAT: Milkweed family (including milkvines).

WHAT THE ADULTS EAT: Nectar.

GARDENING SUGGESTIONS: Milkweeds, especially Mexican milkweed.

ABUNDANCE: Queens are usually common; Soldiers rare to uncommon. Both fly throughout the year southward, moving northward as warm weather progresses.

ETC.: Although the migratory movements of Monarchs is understood in quite some detail, that of Queens is completely unknown. Each year, in October and November, huge but variable numbers of Queens move southward through extreme south Texas into Mexico. Do at least some of these Queens come from the northern reaches of the Queen's range — from Colorado and Kansas? We don't know. Once the Queens move into northern Mexico, do they simply disperse into the countryside, or are there overwintering aggregations, à la Monarchs? This is one of many butterfly mysteries that have yet to be solved.

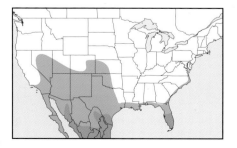

● **Range of Queen.**
● **Range where both Queen and Soldier are found.**

Opposite: A Queen nectaring at beach sunflower. *Top:* Topside of nectaring Queen. *Top inset:* Queen caterpillar. *Bottom:* A Soldier nectaring at lantana. *Bottom inset:* Soldier caterpillar.

Beamers   No. of species: 2

LENGTH OF FOREWING: ━━━━━━━━━

HOW TO KNOW THEM: The iridescent turquoise beams, on the wings and on the body, signal that these are beamers. If you miss the beams, then perhaps their large size (for skippers) or their allover cobalt blue iridescence may catch your attention. Beamers are mainly tropical, but wonderfully, there are two species that enter (just barely) the United States.

WHERE THEY LIVE: Mangrove Skippers inhabit mangrove swamps, spilling out into adjacent areas. Guava Skippers are found at the edges of, and in openings within, tropical and subtropical woodlands.

WHAT THE CATERPILLARS EAT: Red mangrove for Mangrove Skipper. Guava for Guava Skipper.

WHAT THE ADULTS EAT: Nectar.

GARDENING SUGGESTIONS: Mangrove Skipper caterpillars are unlikely to be in your garden unless you live in a houseboat. You can try enticing the adults by planting morning glories, bougainvilleas, or lantanas. Guava Skippers are very possible in

your garden in extreme southern Texas. Plant guavas for the caterpillars and mistflowers for the adults.

ABUNDANCE: Both species of North American beamers fly throughout the year but are usually uncommon.

🔘 **Range of Guava Skipper.**
⚫ **Range of Mangrove Skipper.**

Opposite: A Mangrove Skipper nectaring at morning-glory. ***Above:*** A Guava Skipper nectaring at mistflower.

Silver-spotted Skipper   No. of species: I

LENGTH OF FOREWING: ━━━━━━━━━━

HOW TO KNOW THEM: Even in flight, one can see the flashing silver spot on the underside of the hindwing of this large and powerfully flying skipper.

WHERE THEY LIVE: A great variety of open areas, including roadsides, gardens, and vacant fields.

WHAT THE CATERPILLARS EAT: Black locust, indigo, and other legumes.

WHAT THE ADULTS EAT: Nectar.

GARDENING SUGGESTIONS: In much of the country, this is the spread-wing skipper that is most probable in your garden. Try butterfly pea or indigos.

ABUNDANCE: Mainly uncommon to common, flying through much of the warmer months.

ETC.: The closely related Zestos Skipper is found only on the Florida Keys. Like almost all the butterflies of the Florida Keys, its numbers have declined precipitously over the past twenty-five years, and its future survival is in doubt.

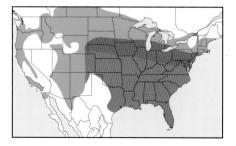

● **Range of Silver-spotted Skipper, I flight.**
● **Range of Silver-spotted Skipper, 2 flights.**
● **Range of Silver-spotted Skipper, 3 flights.**

Opposite: A Silver-spotted Skipper nectaring at zinnia. *Above:* A Silver-spotted Skipper obtaining salts at gravel.

Longtails   No. of species: 6

LENGTH OF FOREWING: ────────────

HOW TO KNOW THEM: Large skippers with long tails are certain to be longtails. The most widespread species, Long-tailed Skipper, has brilliant blue-green iridescence on its topside. Dorantes Longtail, in south Florida, lacks the iridescence above.

WHERE THEY LIVE: Woodland edges, open fields, and disturbed situations for Long-tailed Skipper; open woodlands, gardens, and thorn scrub for others.

WHAT THE CATERPILLARS EAT: A wide variety of legumes.

WHAT THE ADULTS EAT: Nectar.

GARDENING SUGGESTIONS: Longtails are likely to be in your garden. Try garden beans or butterfly pea.

ABUNDANCE: Long-tailed Skipper is common to abundant in south Florida, flying all year. As the season progresses, Long-tailed Skippers move northward but remain scarce at the northern limits of their range. Dorantes Longtail is also common to abundant in south Florida, and southern Texas, but it doesn't move northward so strongly. White-striped Longtail ranges almost to Houston. Brown, Teleus, and Zilpa Longtails are restricted to south Texas. Mottled Longtail has been known to stray into south Texas.

ETC.: Long-tailed Skipper is one of the few butterflies considered to be minor agricultural pests. Others include Giant Swallowtail and Cabbage White.

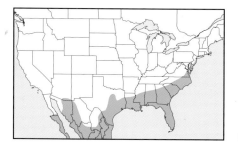

● **Range of longtails.**

Opposite: A White-striped Longtail nectaring at mistflower. ***Top:*** Mottled Longtail. ***Bottom:*** Long-tailed Skipper.

Checkered-Skippers   No. of species: 8

LENGTH OF FOREWING: ━━━━

HOW TO KNOW THEM: The checkered-skippers are black and white packets of energy. Zooming this way and that, they sometimes try one's patience when attempting to get good looks at them. All of these eight species are very similar. In fact, Common Checkered-Skipper is virtually indistinguishable from White Checkered-Skipper. Other species include Grizzled Skipper, as well as Desert, Mountain, Small, Tropical, and Two-banded checkered skippers.

WHERE THEY LIVE: Common Checkered-Skipper, by far the most common and wide-spread, is found in many open situations, including disturbed habitats. Some of the other species live in more specialized habitats, including mountain meadows, and thorn scrub.

WHAT THE CATERPILLARS EAT: The most common species eat mallow family plants. Other species eat cinquefoils.

WHAT THE ADULTS EAT: Nectar.

GARDENING SUGGESTIONS: Possible in your garden. Try hollyhocks, cheeseweed, various globemallows and checkermallows.

ABUNDANCE: In the South, checkered-skippers are mainly common to abundant, flying throughout warm weather. Farther north they are mainly rare to uncommon, flying either in a single brood, or occurring mainly as immigrants, depending upon the species.

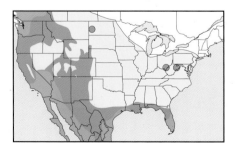

● **Range of Common Checkered-Skipper.**

● **Range of checkered-skippers other than Common.**

● **Range where both Common Checkered-Skippers and other checkered-skippers are found.**

Opposite: White Checkered-Skipper. ***Above:*** Desert Checkered-Skipper.

Cloudywings & Duskywings   No. of species: 9 + 19

LENGTH OF FOREWING: ───────────

HOW TO KNOW THEM: We now enter territory where many fear to tread, the world of LBJs ("little brown jobs"). Cloudywings and duskywings are both medium-sized spread-wing skippers that are mainly brown. The best way to distinguish the two groups is to look at the background brown color. Cloudywings are an even brown, whereas duskywings are highly mottled.

WHERE THEY LIVE: Given the diversity that comes with 28 species, these butterflies are found in a great variety of habitats.

WHAT THE CATERPILLARS EAT: Cloudywings eat legumes, especially beggarweeds and clovers. Most duskywings eat oaks or various legumes, but some eat other plants, too.

WHAT THE ADULTS EAT: Nectar.

GARDENING SUGGESTIONS: Duskywings in particular are very possible in your garden as adult visitors. Small native oaks in your garden couldn't hurt, especially since they are also foodplants for many other kinds of butterflies.

ABUNDANCE: Many of the species are common to abundant. Flight season varies according to species and location.

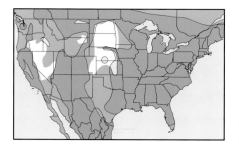

ETC.: Wild Indigo Duskywings historically ate wild indigo, but now commonly eat crown vetch, an alien plant introduced for erosion control.

● **Range of cloudywings.**
● **Range of duskywings.**
● **Range where both are found.**

Opposite: Southern Cloudywing at crown vetch. *Opposite inset:* Desert Cloudywing caterpillar.
Above: Wild Indigo Duskywing nectaring at Canada thistle.

Skipperlings   No. of species: 5

LENGTH OF FOREWING: ▬▬▬▬▬

HOW TO KNOW THEM: Halfway between the spread-wing skippers and the grass-skippers are the skipperlings. On their underwings most species have an unusual spot pattern that brings to mind a miniature fritillary (see the Arctic Skipper photo above), although Russet Skipperling is unmarked on its hindwing.

WHERE THEY LIVE: Arctic Skippers live in moist grassy openings in coniferous and mixed forests. Russet and Four-spotted Skipperlings are found in moist grassy riparian situations. Other skipperlings are found in open oak or pine-oak woodlands.

WHAT THE CATERPILLARS EAT: Grasses.

WHAT THE ADULTS EAT: Nectar.

GARDENING SUGGESTIONS: Adult skipperlings have a real affinity for wild geraniums.

ABUNDANCE: Mainly rare to uncommon, but population density can be rather high in very localized colonies. These species normally have one flight per year, varying with the species. Arctic Skippers fly in late spring, Russet Skipperlings in midsummer, and Many-banded Skipperlings in August (along the Mexican border in Arizona). Chisos Skipperling has bred in Big Bend National Park.

ETC.: The range of Arctic Skippers is circumpolar. In England, where they are endangered, they are called Chequered Skippers.

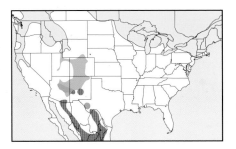

○ **Range of Arctic Skipper.**

● **Range of Russet Skipperling.**

◕ **Range of other skipperlings.**

● **Range where both Russet and other non–Arctic Skipper skipperlings are found.**

Opposite: Arctic Skipperling at wild geranium. **Top:** Russet Skipperling at Richardson's geranium.
Bottom: Four-spotted Skipperling at pinewoods geranium.

Grass-Skippers   No. of species: 118

LENGTH OF FOREWING: ▬▬▬▬

HOW TO KNOW THEM: The LBJs ("little brown jobs") can be trouble, but grass-skippers present a true SOS ("small orange skippers") situation! Calls for help with specific species identifications are likely to go unheeded, but one can fairly easily recognize a butterfly as a grass-skipper. First, their wing shape is really unlike any other butterfly but the skipperlings. Second, they have a characteristic low, rapid, and direct flight. And lastly, when grass-skippers open their wings (which they do fairly frequently), their forewings and hindwings do not move in unison. Thus, when their wings are fully open, the hindwings are held flat, while the forewings are held at a 45° angle (see photo of Fiery Skipper on the next page). Neither spread-wing skippers nor skipperlings exhibit this behavior (giant-skippers do, but those are giants!).

WHERE THEY LIVE: Everywhere (well, almost).

WHAT THE CATERPILLARS EAT: Grasses.

WHAT THE ADULTS EAT: Nectar.

GARDENING SUGGESTIONS: If your property is large enough to include a section with native grasses, this would be good. Little bluestem is a beautiful grass used by many grass-skippers; panic grasses are used by a number of others.

ABUNDANCE: The full spectrum, from abundant to endangered.

● **Range of grass-skippers.**

Opposite: A Juba Skipper nectaring at rabbitbrush. ***Above:*** A male Fiery Skipper nectaring at celosia.

Giant-Skippers   No. of species: 13

LENGTH OF FOREWING: ━━━━━━━━━━

HOW TO KNOW THEM: These are the really big guys of the skipper world. Few people have seen them in the wild. Truth be told, to date, not that many people have looked. The eight species of agave-feeders look very similar to Mojave Giant-Skipper. Species include Arizona, California, Coahuila, Cofaqui, Huachuca, Manfreda, Mary's, Mojave, Orange, Poling's, Strecker's, Ursine, and Yucca giant-skippers.

WHERE THEY LIVE: Yucca grasslands for the yucca-feeders. Mainly rocky deserts with agaves for the agave-feeders.

WHAT THE CATERPILLARS EAT: One group of species eats yuccas, the other group eats agaves. Many of the giant-skippers specialize on just a few, or one, species of plant. For example, Mojave Giant-Skipper caterpillars eat only Utah agaves.

WHAT THE ADULTS EAT: Moisture at mudpuddles. Flowers are not normally visited.

GARDENING SUGGESTIONS: Unlikely to be in your garden, but if you plant yuccas or agaves a stray giant-skipper might find them. And if they don't, the yuccas and agaves will still be incredibly beautiful!

ABUNDANCE: Mostly rare to uncommon. Almost all species have one flight per year. Yucca Giant-Skipper has one spring flight while two other yucca-feeders, Strecker's and Ursine Giant-Skipper fly in mid-summer and late summer, respectively. The agave feeders, such as Mojave Giant-Skipper, fly mainly in September and October.

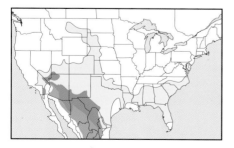

● **Range of yucca-feeding giant-skippers.**
● **Range of agave-feeding giant-skippers.**
● **Range where both are found.**

Opposite: Strecker's Giant-Skipper. *Above:* Habitat for Mojave Giant-Skipper, Mountain Springs, Nevada. Clearly visible are the dead stalks of Utah agave. *Above inset:* Mojave Giant-Skipper.

Scientific Names of Plants and Butterflies

Plant Scientific Names

The common names of plant species are not standardized, and as a result, one book or plant nursery will use one common name while a different book or nursery may well use another name. Although scientific names are not entirely standardized either, they are more consistent than are the common names. For this reason, as an aid to locating pictures or descriptions of plants mentioned in this book, or the plants themselves, scientific names of plants mentioned are provided below. Family names are in roman type and genus and species names are in italics.

Common Name	Scientific Name
Acanthus family	Acanthaceae
Agaves	*Agave*
Utah	*A. utahensis*
Alders	*Alnus*
Alfalfa	*Medicago sativa*
Apache plume	*Fallugia paradoxa*
Ash	*Fraxinus*
Aspens	*Populus*
Aster family	Compositae
Asters	*Aster*
flat-topped white	*A. umbellatus*
leafy-headed	*A. foliaceus*
western	*A. occidentalis*
Bacopa	*Bacopa*
Balloon vine	*Cardiospermum*
Bays	*Persea*
Red	*P. borbonia*
Beans	
garden	*Phaseolus*
Bearberry	*Arctostyphlos uvaursi*
Beard tongue	*Penstemon*
Beggarweeds	*Desmodium*
Bidens	*Bidens*
Bindweed	*Convulvulus*
Birches	*Betula*
Black-eyed Susans	*Rudbeckia*
Blazing-stars	*Liatris*
Bleeding-hearts	*Dicentra*
Blueberries	*Vaccinium*
Blue flag	*Iris versicolor & prismatica*
Bluestem	
little	*Andropogon scoparius*
Bluets	*Houstonia*
Broccoli	*Brassica oleracea*
Buckwheats	*Eriogonum*
sulphur	*E. umbellatum*
Butterfly bush	*Buddleia davidii*
Butterfly pea	*Clitoria mariana*
Cabbage	*Brassica oleracea*
Cassias	*Cassia* (or *Senna*)
Ceanothus	*Ceanothus*
Cedars	Cupressaceae
Cedar	
Atlantic white	*Chamaecyparis thyoides*
eastern red	*Juniperus virginiana*
incense	*Calocedrus decurrens*
Celosia	*Celosia*
Cevallia	
stinging	*Cevallia sinuata*
Checkermallows	*Sidalcea*
Cheeseweed	*Malva neglecta*
Cherry	
black	*Prunus serotina*
Chinese-houses	*Collinsea*
Chinquapin	*Castanopsis*
Cinquefoils	*Potentilla*
Citrus family	Rutaceae

Common Name	Scientific Name
Cheese-shrub	*Morinda royac*
Clematis	*Clematis*
Clovers	*Trifolium*
white	*T. repens*
Cologania	
downy	*Cologania angustifolia*
Composite	Compositae
Coneflowers	*Echinacea*
Coontie	*Zamia pumila*
Coyote mint	*Monardella odoratissima*
Croton	
Narrow-leaved	*Croton linearis*
Crown vetch	*Coronilla varia*
Crucifers	Cruciferae
Cudweeds	*Gnaphalium*
Currants	*Ribes*
Cycads	Cycadaceae
Cypress	
Sargent's	*Cupressus sargentii*
Daisy	
ox-eyed	*Chrysanthemum leucanthemum*
Dandelions	*Taraxacum*
Deerweed	*Lotus scoparius*
Docks	*Rumex*
Dogbanes	*Apocynum*
Dudleya	*Dudleya*
canyon	*D. cymosa*
Elms	*Ulmus*
Fairy-duster	
Baja	*Calliandra californica*
Fennel	*Foeniculum vulgare*
Figs	*Ficus*
short-leaved	*F. citrifolia*
Fleabanes	*Erigeron*
Fogfruits	*Lippia*
Geranium	
pinewoods	*Geranium caespitosum*
Richardson's	*G. richardsonii*
wild	*G. maculatum*
Gerardias	*Gerardia*
Glassworts	*Salicornia*
Globemallows	*Sphaeralcea*
Goldenrods	*Solidago*
Gooseberries	*Ribes*
Grasses	Poaceae
Guava	*Psidium guajava*
Hackberries	*Celtis*
Heliotrope	*Heliotropium*
Hercules' club	*Zanthoxylum clava-herculis*
Honeysuckle	
twinberry	*Lonicera involucrate*
Hoptree	*Ptelea trifoliata*

Indian paintbrushes *Castilleja*
Indigos *Amorpha*
  False *A. californica*

Joe-pye weed *Eupatorium maculatum*
  et al.
Junipers *Juniperus*

Kidneywood *Eysenhardtia*
Knotweeds *Polygonum*

Lantana *Lantana*
Laurel family Laurelaceae
Lavender
  desert *Hyptis emoryi*
Legumes Leguminosae
Lemon *Citrus limon*
Lily
  oriental *Lilium rubrum*
Lime
  wild *Zanthoxylum fagara*
Locust
  black *Robina pseudacacia*
Lupines *Lupinus*

Mallow family Malvaceae
Mangrove
  black *Avicennia germinans*
  red *Rhizophora mangle*
Maypop *Passiflora incarnata*
Mesquites *Prosopsis*
Milkvines *Sarcostemma*
Milkweeds *Asclepias*
  common *A. syriaca*
  Mexican *A. curassavica*
  narrow-leaved *A. fascicularis*
  orange *A. tuberosa*
  purple *A. purpurascens*
  showy *A. speciosa*
  swamp *A. incarnata*
  whorled *A. verticillata*
Mistflowers *Eupatorium*
Mistletoes *Phoradendron*
Monkey flowers *Mimulus*
Morning-glories *Ipomoea*
Mustard family Cruciferae

Nasturtium *Tropaelum majus*
Nettles *Urticae*
Nettle
  false *Boehmeria cylindrica*

Oaks *Quercus*
  canyon *Q. chrysolepis*
  Gambel's *Q. gambelii*

Panic grasses *Panicum*
Parsley *Petroselinum crispum*
Parsley family Umbelliferae
Passion vines *Passiflora*
  Blue *P. caerulea*
  Corky-stemmed *P. suberosa*
  Tagua *P. foetida*
Pawpaw *Asimina*
Pearly everlastings *Anaphalis*
Peas *Pisum*
Pellitory *Parietaria judaica*
Peppergrass *Lepidium*
Phacelias *Phacelia*
Pipevines *Aristolochia*
  California *A. californica*
  Dutchman's *A. macrophylla* (or *durior*)

elegant *A. elegans*
Watson's *A. watsoni*
Pines *Pinus*
  ponderosa *Pinus ponderosa*
Plantain *Plantago*
Plum
  beach *Prunus maritima*
Poplars *Populus*
Pussypaws *Calyptridium umbellatum*
Pussytoes *Antennaria*

Rabbitbrush *Chrysothamnus nauseosus*
Ragwort
  Round-leaved *Senecio obovatus*
Rock cresses *Arabis*
Ruellias *Ruella*

Saltbush *Atriplex*
Sassafras *Sassafras albidum*
Sedges *Carex*
Seepwillow *Baccharis glutinosa*
Sennas *Cassia* or *Senna*
  Chapman's *C. chapmani*
  Christmas *C. bicapsularis*
Shrimp plants *Beloperone*
  green *Blechum brownei*
Sicklepod *Arabis canadensis*
Silverleafs *Leucophyllum*
Snapdragons *Antirrhinum*
Snapdragon family Scrophulariacea
Snowberries *Symphoricarpus*
Spicebush *Lindera benzoin*
Stonecrop *Sedum*
Sunflowers *Helianthus*
  beach *H. debilis*
Sunflower
  Mexican *Tithonia rotundifolia*
Sweet bay *Magnolia virginiana*
Sweetbush *Bebbia juncea*

Tagua passion vine *Passiflora foetida*
Tamarind
  wild *Tamarindus indica*
Tecate cypress *Cupressus forbesii*
Thistles *Cirsium*
  Canada *C. arvense*
  swamp *C. muticum*
  yellow *C. horridulum*
Thoroughwort
  white-bracted *Eupatorium leucolepis*
Thyme *Thymus vulgaris*
Tulip-tree *Liriodendron tulipifera*
Turtlehead *Chelone glabra*

Verbena family Verbenaceae
Vetches *Vicia*
Violets *Viola*
  birdfoot *V. pedata*

Water hyssop
  smooth *Bacopa monnieri*
Willows *Salix*
Wood sorrel *Oxalis*

Yerba santa
  sticky *Eriodictyon californicum*
Yuccas *Yucca*

Zinnia *Zinnia*
  orange sparkler *Z. angustifolia*

Butterfly Scientific Names

Although the common names of butterflies are well on their way to being standardized (most recent butterfly books use the North American Butterfly Association list, available at the NABA website, www.naba.org), there are still older books in circulation that use nonstandard names. The following list may be helpful if you are using one of these older books. Family names are in roman type and genus and species names are in italics.

Common Name	Scientific Name
Admirals	
Lorquin's	*Limenitis lorquini*
Red	*Vanessa atalanta*
Red-spotted	*Limenitis arthemis*
Weidemeyer's	*L. weidemeyerii*
White	*L. arthemis arthemis*
Alpines	
Common	*Erebia epipsodea*
Theano	*E. theano*
Vidler's	*E. vidleri*
Arctics	
Chryxus	*Oeneis chryxus*
Melissa	*O. melissa*
Atala	*Eumaeus atala*
Azures	
Appalachian	*Celastrina neglectamajor*
Dusky	*C. nigra*
Spring	*C. ladon*
Beamer	*Phocides*
Blues	
Acmon	*Plebejus acmon*
Arrowhead	*Glaucopsyche piasus*
Boisduval's	*Plebejus icarioides*
Ceraunus	*Hemiargus ceraunus*
Greenish	*Plebejus saepiolus*
Marine	*Hemiargus marina*
Melissa	*Lycaeides melissa*
Reakirt's	*Hemiargus isola*
Silvery	*Glaucopsyche lygdamus*
Sonoran	*Philotes sonorensis*
Bluewing	
Mexican	*Myscelia ethusa*
Brown	
Eyed	*Satyrodes eurydice*
Buckeyes	
Common	*Junonia coenia*
Mangrove	*J. evarete*
Tropical	*J. genoveva*
Checkered-Skippers	
Common	*Pyrgus communis*
Desert	*P. philetas*
White	*P. albescens*
Checkerspots	
Baltimore	*Euphydryas phaeton*
Black	*Thessalia cyneas*
Chinati	*T. chinatiensis*
Edith's	*Euphydryas editha*
Fulvia	*Thessalia fulvia*
Gillett's	*Euphydryas gillettii*
Gorgone	*Chlosyne gorgone*
Harris'	*C. harrisii*
Leanira	*Thessalia leanira*
Sagebrush	*Chlosyne acastus*
Theona	*Thessalia theona*
Variable	*Euphydryas chalcedona*
Cloudywings	
Desert	*Achalarus casica*
Southern	*Thorybes bathyllus*
Commas	
Green	*Polygonia faunus*
Hoary	*P. gracilis*
Coppers	
American	*Lycaena phlaeas*
Blue	*L. heteronea*
Dorcas	*L. dorcas*
Lilac-bordered	*L. nivalis*
Purplish	*L. helloides*
Ruddy	*L. rubidus*
Tailed	*L. arota*
Crescents	
Field	*Phyciodes campestris*
Northern	*P. selenis*
Pearl	*P. tharos*
Phaon	*P. phaon*
Texan	*P. texana*
Daggerwings	
Many-banded	*Marpesia chiron*
Ruddy	*M. petreus*
Dogfaces	
California	*Colias eurydice*
Southern	*C. cesonia*
Duskywing	
Wild Indigo	*Erynnis baptisiae*
Elfins	
Brown	*Callophrys augustinus*
Hoary	*C. polios*
Western Pine	*C. eryphon*
Emperor	
Tawny	*Asterocampa clyton*
Empress Leilia	*A. leilia*
Fritillaries	
Coronis	*Speyeria coronis*
Diana	*S. diana*
Great Spangled	*S. cybele*
Gulf	*Agraulis vanillae*
Meadow	*Boloria bellona*
Mormon	*Speyeria mormonia*
Nokomis	*S. nokomis*
Pacific	*Boloria epithore*
Purplish	*B. montinus*
Silver-bordered	*B. selene*
Unsilvered	*Speyeria adiaste*
Giant-Skippers	
Mojave	*Agathymus alliae*
Strecker's	*Megathymus streckeri*
Ursine	*M. ursus*
Yucca	*M. yuccae*
Giant-Sulphur	*Phoebis*
Hairstreaks	
Acadian	*Satyrium acadica*
Colorado	*Hypaurotis crysalus*
Coral	*Satyrium titus*
Edwards'	*S. edwardsii*
Golden	*Habrodais grunus*
Gray	*Strymon melinus*
Great Purple	*Atlides halesus*
Hedgerow	*Satyrium saepium*
Hessel's	*Callophrys hesseli*
Juniper	*C. gryneus*
Silver-banded	*Chlorostrymon simaethis*
Harvester	*Feniseca tarquinius*
Heliconians	
Julia	*Dryas iulia*

Zebra	*Heliconius charithonia*
Kite-Swallowtail	*Eurytides*
Ladies	
American	*Vanessa virginiensis*
Painted	*V. cardui*
West Coast	*V. annabella*
Leafwings	
Florida	*Anaea floridalis*
Holy	*Zaretis ellops*
Tropical	*Anaea aidea*
Longtails	
Mottled	*Typhedanus undulatus*
White-striped	*Chioides catillus*
Malachite	*Siproeta stelenes*
Marbles	
Large	*Euchloe ausonides*
Olympia	*E. olympia*
Metalmarks	
Arizona	*Calephelis arizonensis*
Mormon	*Apodemia mormo*
Nais	*A. nais*
Northern	*Calephelis borealis*
Palmer's	*Apodemia palmeri*
Rawson's	*Calephelis rawsoni*
Rounded	*C. perditalis*
Swamp	*C. muticum*
Wright's	*C. wrighti*
Monarch	*Danaus plexippus*
Mourning Cloak	*Nymphalis antiopa*
Oranges	
Sleepy	*Eurema nicippe*
Tailed	*E. proterpia*
Orangetips	
Desert	*Anthocharis cethura*
Falcate	*A. midea*
Sara	*A. sara*
Patches	
Bordered	*Chlosyne lacinia*
California	*C. californica*
Crimson	*C. janais*
Parnassians	
Clodius	*Parnassius clodius*
Phoebus	*P. phoebus*
Peacock	
White	*Anartia jatrophae*
Pearly-eye	
Northern	*Enodia anthedon*
Pixie	
red-bordered	*Melanis pixe*
Purple	
Red-spotted	*Limenitis arthemis astyanax*
Purplewing	
Dingy	*Eunica monima*
Pygmy-Blue	
Western	*Brephidium exile*
Queen	*Danaus gilippus*
Question Mark	*Polygonia interrogationis*
Ringlet	
Common	*Coenonympha tullia*
Satyrs	
Carolina	*Hermeuptychia sosybius*
Georgia	*Neonympha areolata*
Mitchell's	*N. michellii*
Nabokov's	*Cyllopsis pyracmon*
Red	*Megisto rubricata*
Scrub-Hairstreaks	
Bartram's	*Strymon acis*

Mallow	*S. istapa*
Martial	*S. martialis*
Skippers	
Arctic	*Carterocephalus palaemon*
Fiery	*Hylephila phyleus*
Guava	*Phocides polybius*
Juba	*Hesperia juba*
Long-tailed	*Urbanus proteus*
Mangrove	*Phocides pigmalion*
Ocola	*Panoquina ocola*
Silver-spotted	*Epargyreus clarus*
Zabulon	*Poanes zabulon*
Zestos	*Epargyreus zestos*
Skipperlings	
Four-spotted	*Piruna polingi*
Many-spotted	*P. cingo*
Russet	*P. pirus*
Snout	
American	*Libytheana carinenta*
Soldier	*Danaus erisimus*
Sulphurs	
Clouded	*Colias philodice*
Cloudless	*Phoebis sennae*
Dainty	*Nathalis iole*
Large Orange	*Phoebis agarithe*
Mead's	*Colias meadii*
Orange	*C. eurytheme*
Pink-edged	*C. interior*
Swallowtails	
Anise	*Papilio zelicaon*
Black	*P. polixenes*
Canadian Tiger	*P. canadensis*
Eastern Tiger	*P. glaucus*
Giant	*P. cresphontes*
Palamedes	*P. palamedes*
Pale	*P. eurymedon*
Pipevine	*Battus philenor*
Polydamas	*B. polydamas*
Schaus'	*Papilio schausi*
Spicebush	*P. troilus*
Two-tailed	*P. multicaudata*
Western Tiger	*P. rutulus*
Zebra	*Eurytides marcellus*
Tailed-Blues	
Eastern	*Everes comyntas*
Western	*E. amyntula*
Tortoiseshells	
California	*Nymphalis californica*
Compton	*N. vaualbum*
Milbert's	*N. milberti*
Viceroy	*Limenitis archippus*
Whites	
Becker's	*Pontia beckerii*
Cabbage	*Pieris rapae*
Checkered	*Pontia protodice*
Chiracahua	*Neophasia terlootii*
Mustard	*Pieris napi*
Pine	*Neophasia menapia*
Western	*Pontia occidentalis*
West Virginia	*Pieris virginiensis*
Wood-Nymph	
Common	*Cercyonis pegala*
Wood-Satyr	
Little	*Megisto cymela*
Yellows	
Barred	*Eurema daira*
Dina	*E. dina*
Little	*E. lisa*
Mexican	*E. mexicana*

Index of Plants

Index of Butterflies

Selected Bibliography

Below is a select list of books that provide useful information about butterflies. Each of the books was selected not just for the quality of information it provides, but for its currency—every one was published after 1990.

Allen, T. *The Butterflies of West Virginia.* University of Pittsburgh Press, 1997.

Bailowitz, R.A. and Brock, J.P. *Butterflies of Southeastern Arizona.* Tucson: Sonoran Arthropod Studies Institute, 1991.

Glassberg, J. *Butterflies through Binoculars: Boston-New York-Washington.* New York: Oxford University Press, 1993.

Glassberg, J. *Butterflies through Binoculars: The East.* New York: Oxford University Press, 1999.

Glassberg, J. *Butterflies through Binoculars: The West.* New York: Oxford University Press, 2001.

Glassberg, J. , Minno, M.C., and Calhoun, J.V. *Butterflies through Binoculars: Florida.* New York: Oxford University Press, 2000.

Gochfeld, M. and Burger, J. *Butterflies of New Jersey.* Rutgers University Press, 1997.

Iftner, D.C., Shuey, J.A. and Calhoun, J.V. *The Butterflies and Skippers of Ohio.* Columbus: The Ohio State University, 1992.

Minno, M.C. and Emmel, T.C. *Butterflies of the Florida Keys.* Gainesville: Scientific Publishers, 1993.

Opler, P.A. *A Field Guide to Eastern Butterflies.* Houghton-Mifflin, 1992.

Opler, P.A. *A Field Guide to Western Butterflies.* Houghton-Mifflin, 1999.

Pyle, R.M. *Chasing Monarchs.* Boston: Houghton-Mifflin, 1999.

Stewart, B., Brodkin, P. and Brodkin, H. *Butterflies of Arizona.* Tucson: West Coast Lady Press, 2001.

Sutton, P.T. and Sutton C. *How to Spot a Butterfly.* Boston: Houghton-Mifflin, 1999.

Tveten, J. and Tveten, G. *Butterflies of Houston.* Austin: University of Texas Press, 1996.

Wauer, R. *Butterflies of West Texas Parks and Preserves.* Texas Tech University Press, 2002.

Weber, L. *Butterflies of the North Woods.* Duluth: Kollath-Stensaas Publishing, 2001.

North American Butterfly Association

The North American Butterfly Association (NABA) is a nonprofit membership association whose mission is to increase public enjoyment and conservation of butterflies. NABA publishes the full-color quarterly *American Butterflies* and the color quarterly newsletter *Butterfly Gardener*, and runs the NABA 4th of July Butterfly Count Program. Its extensive website, www.naba.org, includes the Butterflies I've Seen database, allowing users to track and map all of their butterfly sightings, free butterfly gardening brochures, an on-line butterfly guide and discussion groups, as well as pages detailing field trip and other local information for many of the more than thirty NABA chapters existing as of this writing. If you are unable to visit the website, write to NABA, 4 Delaware Rd., Morristown, NJ 07960, for membership information, or call 800-503-2290 (membership inquiries only).